# Itch

# I*tch*

Steven Seidenberg

For Paul and Ben —
In anticipation of future conversation —
12/9/13

Foreword by Andrew Joron

RAW ArT PRESS
Pittsburg, California

ISBN 978-0-9819534-5-8

1. Literature  2. Literary Nonfiction
3. Experimental Narrative

Library of Congress Control Number 2013950098




RAW ArT PRESS
*Experimental Prose Series*
Trena Machado, Publisher


Front Cover Art: Steven Seidenberg
Cover Design: Inez Machado

## PUBLISHER'S NOTE

*Itch*, a manuscript, original in structure, language and conceptual scope—a mix of poetry and philosophy—came to my attention. I was intrigued by the lyrical rhythm of the sentences, as each paragraph launched to the next by an open-ended ellipsis and by a narrator, waking one morning, confronted by a problem difficult to name. As the narrator works with and is pulled into *the problem*, we are brought into the center of consciousness and go through the process of exploring identity, self and the world by way of the senses and cognition. The narrator dealing with the whole of everything through *the problem's* lens brings us into the story of philosophy. For me, this kind of narrative was a new thing, not only in its unique synthesis, but for the beauty of its language. RAW ArT PRESS enthusiastically offers *Itch* as a contribution in the conversation on narrative.

Trena Machado

## FOREWORD

### *The Unbearable Itchiness of Being*

This is a book of First Philosophy: an attempt, startling in this era when pure thought is understood to be overdetermined by social and linguistic factors, to discover the meaning of being in the world through the motions of thought alone.

The motions of the mind are not the same as the motions of (socially mediated) language. There is a resistance, a tension, between them, as becomes evident in Steven Seidenberg's monologue, *Itch*. The mind's momentum, driven from below by the urgencies of flesh and from above the demands of society, is further augmented and diminished by the viscous flow of language systems. These systems themselves issue from social systems but then become semi-autonomous, pulling the already fraught mind into a strangely inhuman, perhaps interstellar, coordinate system—into a new order of being, made up of the uncanny relations that exist between those *present absences* of signs. Thus, the subject of *Itch* is itself a "present absence" that, in attempting to conjure and confirm its own being through language, finds itself distorted by that very language, receding infinitely into the mirror-worlds of words.

Language, like the rest of being, offers only a never-ending series of conditions, thwarting at every turn the search for an unconditional identity. A glimpse of the Unconditional may be had in the speechlessness of a mystical state, or in the attempt to "say the unsayable" through the music of poetry. Discursive prose, however, can approach only the idea, not the reality, of the Unconditional. The body of discursive prose suffers from an itch that cannot be scratched.

As finite beings, we are condemned to desire. The wholeness that we seek, however, would mean the dissolution of our finitude, its vanishment into infinity. The word "itch," however, connotes a physical rather than a spiritual desire. It is a superficial yet insistent tension, similar to pain—uncannily so—yet not painful. It is bothersome in the manner of a minor neurosis, a recurrent and nettlesome thought. Quelling an itch brings a relief that can hardly be compared to a reunion with the Unconditional; at best, such quelling restores a bodily equilibrium. And yet: such equilibrium is itself a fictive and unattainable state. The living body must constantly endure a swarm of sensations; indeed, the word "irritation" was once a synonym for sensation. To live is to itch.

This itch also occurs on the membrane of the page, as the irritation of writing upon a (perhaps previously blissful) blankness. It is the itch of consciousness at the interface between subject and object. Such an itch represents the discomfiture of the mind's accommodation to the body, and to the (always foreign) words it must use to express this discomfiture. Yet, although every language is a foreign language, nothing other than language allows the animal to jump out of its skin, into a new and expansive ghost-body. Is this newly evolved, present-absent body also subject to the itch of being?

The answer, in this case, appears to be no: here, language is treated as a transparent medium that provides a view of the motions of a mind in turmoil. The problem of *Itch* is to resolve the irritation, not only of being, but of being a self—a thinking being—in a world that may be negatively defined as not-self. In all of *Itch's* iterations of the irritations of being, however, the not-self of language is never at issue. As surely as the subject of *Itch* possesses an embodied mind that is opaquely subject to irritation, he possesses a clear, and therefore non-irritating, language with which to consider his plight. Thus, the utopia of a transparent self-relation is already erected, in this struggle to achieve self-realization, at the level of language, but because it is transparent—or at least assumed to be so—it remains an invisible victory.

Nonetheless, the structures of language bring their own conditionality to this mind's search for an unconditional (itch-free) relation to itself and the world. In particular, the communicative structure of language becomes palpable in the transaction between first and second person: here, the "I" constantly addresses a "you," the latter given full recognition as a second self and serving as a mute witness, a receiver of the signals emitted by the sender-self.

Now, the problem of self-consciousness—in which the subject must transform itself into an object in order to know itself, in the process becoming something other than itself, and thereby losing rather than gaining itself as self—has often enough been reconstructed in terms of intersubjectivity. In this approach, the human subject necessarily enters into a sociolinguistic circle with other subjects; each subject, while remaining the same as itself, is variously construed in the first person (as self), second person (as the object of direct communication), and third person (as the object of indirect communication). By entering this circle, the subject is able to recognize itself as an object (of communication)—and the additional problem of how the self recognizes itself as its own special object within a manifold of contingent objects is solved by routing such recognition through the intersubjective medium of language.

As the British philosopher Peter Dews writes, in his essay on self-consciousness and modernity, "Linguistic mastery of the use of the term 'I' involves the—at least implicit—knowledge that conscious states which I attribute to myself in the first person can be attributed to me, as an entity identifiable by others through my physically observable features, in the third. The meaning of the term 'I' is determined by its interchangeability, according to viewpoint, within a system of deictic terms."[1] In *Itch* , the "I"'s recurrent petition of a "you" would seem to fulfill this function of generating self-consciousness by means of an intersubjective language-game. It should be noted that this game does not require the actual presence of an Other, but merely the positing of an Imaginary Friend. Here, the conjunction of subject and object is guaranteed by the structure of language—a structuring as basic to consciousness as the Kantian categories of space, time, and causality.

At the same time, *Itch* is not a dialogue but a monologue: the subject's sense, frequently iterated in the text, that "there's something missing" does not refer to the "you"—whose position as witness or auditor is taken for granted here—but to an opacity situated beyond those transparent language-structures of which the "you" and the "I" are simply a part. The opacity belongs, not to language, but to the *experience* of the subject as a subject-of-being-in-the-world. The monologue, while often addressed to a "you," is conducted as a *self-interrogation* concerning the content and limits of experience itself. The itch serves to delimit the embodied mind, but if this limit were removed (if the itch were to be scratched), then what?

(For *Itch* is finally a story of desire: not of the subject's desire for the Other or any other object as limit-condition, but of desire for that which transcends all limits, amounting to a limitless desire, a desire for desire itself. To scratch that itch, then, would be to arrive at a state of being beyond the imposition of limits; yet how could such a breakthrough lead to anything but further incitement by a kind of being that cannot contain itself, a kind of meta-itch?)

The itch, as it serves to delimit, thus stands for the resistance of being to itself. This is what ultimately motivates the thought-narrative of *Itch*: namely, that which resists thought. *Itch* undertakes the attempt to think (or to be) something missing from thought (or being), something that escapes signification entirely. The story starts in the middle, when the "I" already has attained at least a preliminary phase of self-constitution, a phase secured by the forms of address used in intersubjective communication. Having come this far, the "I" is led to declare, echoing the catchword of Marxist-Utopian philosopher

Ernst Bloch, that "something is missing [*etwas fehlt*]."

Despite this echo, however, what's missing in terms of *Itch* most resembles the inscrutable Lack that appears as Lacan's *object petit a*, a lack felt most acutely at a psycholinguistic rather than a sociopolitical level (but it would be interesting, in another context, to explore the affinities between Lacan's Freud-inspired concept and Bloch's Marx-inspired one). Lacan redefined his concept of the *objet a* many times, but one useful general definition is provided by the Lacanian analyst Bruce Fink, who writes that the *object a "is the leftover of that process of constituting an object, the scrap that evades the grasp of symbolization"* [emphasis in original]. It is a reminder that there is something else, something perhaps lost, perhaps yet to be found."[2] This definition may be supplemented with Žižek's observation that "the subject is nothing but the impossibility of its own signifying representation"—the empty place opened up in the symbolic order by the failure to constitute itself as its own object. Žižek furthermore argues that the subject's attempt to reflect itself within a signifying chain "ultimately always fails—any positive mark included in the series could never successfully represent/reflect the empty space of the inscription of marks. *It is, however, this very failure as such which 'constitutes' the space of inscription. . . . [T]he very act of reflection as failed constitutes retroactively that which eludes it* [emphasis added]."[3] The subject's own desire for it-knows-not-what is provoked and confirmed by that unfillable desire, the "little a," within the "big A" or Autre of the symbolic order; in the mutuality of this lack, this failure to positively account for their own foundation, both subject and object are retroactively founded.

Yet, what's missing in *Itch* is never conclusively identified as a foundational moment, but only as the limit of awareness. As the narrator puts it, "The boundary I speak of—that I was made *aware* of by the sense of what was missing from the world I *could* receive—is of a different order; not an absence one can vitiate by granting its necessity, but that one could fill up without acceding to its terms." Nonetheless, inasmuch as what's missing comes to be identified with limitation itself, and since awareness, including self-consciousness, is produced by the internal delimitating of being, it is fair to say that the foundational effect of something like the *objet a* radiates its darkness throughout the narrative.

The narrative ends as it began—in the middle; necessarily so, for a limitless line is composed only of midpoints. While the narrator's predicament is not transcended, a "new beginning," a feeling of renewed purpose is attained on the last page. This conclusion could well have been placed at the beginning of the book—for the book undertakes precisely the quest that the narrator announces at its end: "first off to locate the itch—to parse its affectations—and finally move to the world. . . *to move the world* by proffering *a scratch. . . ."*

Andrew Joron
Berkeley, California, 2014

---

[1] Peter Dews, "Modernity, Self-Consciousness, and the Scope of Philosophy," in Dews, *The Limits of Disenchantment: Essays on Contemporary European Philosophy* (London: Verso, 1995), p. 176.

[2] Bruce Fink, *The Lacanian Subject* (Princeton, NJ: Princeton University Press, 1995), p. 94.

[3] Slavoj Žižek, *For They Know Not What They Do* (London, Verso, 1991), p. 86.

# I*tch*

Many failed attempts. Perhaps this is the first. Of my many failed attempts, perhaps this is the first. The first in what will soon appear a series of such failures—surrendered to the obloquy of having yet to happen, or having happened...I say surrendered, and I say attempt, the language of a game which attempts...I say the saying and the saying says...

φ

Perhaps this is the first of all the many claims to primacy required to claim any claim to primacy a proof, an incidental figurement of problems and procedures near to happening...near to constituting happen*stance* as it stands fore right now...

φ

If this is sure the first where there has not yet been a second...If this attempt to...If this trope yet *amounts* to the surrendered primogeniture of other tropes predicted to surrender sometime soon, then how can one presume to think...to *mean* those varied instances within the nearing preterit and certitude of having passed and purposed themselves into...

φ

If this is sure the first of what I know will soon be many...But that's not where this portent finds its bearing—so its aim. What saying this is first without first having said that this is something...something like...that this that I will soon contrive as something like the subject of...of this and this alone...

φ

What saying this presumes is that its referent is this saying this—the saying that this *saying this* presumes, if it's not clear. One ought not need proclaim that such an act of proclamation is occurring—is *transpiring*—by virtue of the saying *of* it in its present term, but thinking of it so and still adducing it as primary allows that what will follow has since discharged its effects, a shouldering of contraries that I can't yet...can't here...can't yet to here abide...

φ

One might well think to countenance this sort of vain perversity—and the speaker thus inveigled to presentiment by the pose—in hopes that such regard could thereby supervene the parallax through which this dreary précis is ostensively reviewed, and I have—or will admit to—no clear motive or intention to do otherwise; one *might* do so, but why take on the trouble of resisting so much contrary resolve...

φ

It's not that there's no evidence to justify describing this the first of many failures all the rest of which have yet to be construed, but rather that the aftermath that *this* failure maintains vows neither to be recently accomplished nor begun, a failed attempt by dint of this attempt to claim a first successful failing to...to...It's clear even *to me* you have no reason to be sure...

φ

And do I now—or still, I'll risk—have any sense what pratfall I have since proposed as primary—the first first in the series, as though the very first of all? The first to send me canting down this course without a recourse; to have at once succeeded in the taking of this seeming leave as though it were a trail? Seeming, I declare, to crudely intimate a *truer* drive, a yet unnamed ambition in this...*from* this deftly garrulous repose, this feigned rapport, despite the fact—which you may well have missed—that I've done only that to make it so. Suggested that it's so. That I've done nothing more...have *proffered* nothing more than the suggestion that it's so to make it *seem* so...

φ

If it appears I have a purpose that's unwittingly concealed by my advancement towards fulfillment—towards *arrival* in the form I will uphold—then it's arguably best for me leave off leaving off with it, and forthwith leave off leaving off with it for good. For the good of all concerned, myself not least among them. Neither most, I'll tell you now, although I might be wrong...

φ

Having made countless attempts at an accounting of the countless, each attempt is equally a failure, a dead end. This may well be the first of all such minor supplications, whether you or I will ever come to know it so before...before what will come after this, whatever that that this is—or will by some yet unknown means *become* when it's revealed. Whatever will come after this will make of this before the very first of all my failures in the endless seriatim that will surely follow after, as one conceives the chain of chance arrayed within the bane that set it off...

φ

That failure results from failure and success from success may seem more of a posture than an inference, or a premise proved; one can readily concede success where there seemed failure in the offing and... What matters in *this* instance—this measure of the case in point by pointing to it elsewhere, to the elsewhere it implies, if not unwittingly presumes—is that my many failures to enumerate my failures are enough to countermand what yet appears the *future* failure of the path we've started on...we've started *down*...

φ

Of my many failed attempts to name my many failed attempts, this one, I assure you, has proved to be the very first, so equally convincing my importunate receivers—importunate, no doubt, but no less welcome a contrivance of the form of this address...the address of this form, which is...So equally *concerning* to whomever should accept this affectation of a prelude—of what I hope will someday seem the prelude to a finished tale—is that there are still countless deviations from my purpose still to come...

φ

But if they're still to come, you ask, how does he know they'll happen? Is he the sort of dullard who sees catastrophe at every turn? Alas, it's not for me to blunt the edge of such accusatives—to countenance an ancillary predicate of character that I can't say I wouldn't scorn were I but judge and not accused. I *can* say that the proof of my ill humor won't be found in the veracity of my anticipations—my near *announcement*, if you will, of some last resort. And even this capitulation won't suffice as an appraisal of the stratagems thus strategized, and aiming towards...

φ

The problem has to do with the foreboding I still feel for those same acts that I allege to have completed—to have *left behind*; the rupture, it appears, between my image of...my *reverence for* a series

6

of events I've claimed concluded and the accompanying announce-ment of that imminent catharsis as though it had preceded all the rest *by its design*...

φ

Yes, yes, you say, what of it; who needs this hardly bold expatiation on the evident...the ostensibly *self*-evident paradox of a past presumed preceded by the inherence of its now. The difficulty, I suspect, has *more* to do with this regression to the first of all my inferences—the gist of our acquaintanceship, both in fealty and affray—while the incident such desultory debitage implies is still *in medias res*; that once again the *this* of which I speak can't be identical to this instance of my speaking it, and yet I'm more than willing to proceed with my account...

φ

Perhaps you see this *this* as but a retrospective prologue, a second thought appended to what's first come first—the first into which this appendage leads us, as a pathway; the first that draws our path-way to its finish, as a line. And while I think I've long since shown my sympathy with the argument—even argued it beyond what I imagined the peculiar skills of those who I imagined firstly raised it, whoever you or they may prove to be, or serve to court—in answer I can only say...can only *claim* it's not the case; that the paradox must not...*will* not yield to resolution if I'm to have my way—whether in the end I have my way or somehow, some way don't...

φ

I may not have my way with this or that digression, accepting that my way is not laid out before it's had, but it's still in agreement with those same preconditions that determine what the making of an ought will...*must* avoid if it's to prove desideratum in the end. Again, I am aware of the discordance of this idiom—without, that is, a sense of fore or aft the fore or aft I've started here...this here*in* with—but such awareness does not sway my addled inclination to continue on the way that I've continued in the past...

φ

I've found no way to properly delineate the passage, other than this manifestly inconclusive pose—a pose that hardly *strikes* despite the absence of its obverse, the sense of having up till now eluded all fidelity to posture *or* device. I've come upon this aggregate—or gleaned it *from the whole*—by claiming to describe my breaking free of its arrears, a subtlety of affect even *I* can't adjudge due. As though one might already have concluded that my competence to prosecute the yet unstated point of this reprise is at the limit of what's possible for *any* sort of intellect to prove. Even I, I say again, am fairly sure the confidence this surety suggests is not quite warranted...will be revealed *un*warranted by avowals still to come...

φ

Whatever this state is—this state in which you've found me, which might as well be understood the state in which I'm found—it is by implication the emergence of the whole towards which this pretense of an ego strives. Whatever I'm *suggesting* is the purpose of my purport, the action of purporting it to not yet be complete must be included—must be *signal*—and this is still the *least* that I'd expect myself to show. To *be*, rather. That I'd believe I'm being, whether knowing that I'd been the being-thus that I've become or...or not; such transitives can't be resolved by any *other* means...

φ

Whatever this position now—this truncheon of a pause—it is what it will be, and nothing else, and nothing...It will be nothing more than it will be, it stands to reason, but that it will be more than it's been yet—than it's *become*—reveals another problem in the shape of it's becoming so—it's next capitulation to the open, to the *clear*...

φ

This *it* which I am now and surely will be by default assumes that if I speak of some identity beyond the narrow scope of merely speaking of it so I will be speaking of the same intrinsic speaking out again, that I'll find that I'm speaking of the same I I referred to when referring to the I I've spoken *as* up to this point. Such a spastic torpor can't help but to usurp the soon to seem invariable accidents of agency despite the selfsame difference—the insuperable *exclusion*—of what I'm speaking of from what I speak of *through*, by which I mean the I I seem to point to with the same portentous whimsy I employ in the apparent speaking out I'm speaking now...

φ

Let us say, for the sake of argument...for all it's worth...for the sake of all it's worth...Let us say that we've conceived of no such grand distemper, and so have left off leaving off without a thought to this delay—to the trouble this excursus is attempting to elude, if not yet resolve into a ready aim...

φ

If I were to here suggest that what will happen next, or rather...or at the least...or at the least *and* rather what events that, having happened, I'll soon narrate to an otherwise inconsequent assent...

φ

If I were to here *address* the preface that sits fore this ever tractable look back as though I've always known how it will *turn out*, so presuming the existence of the addressee that you have quite surprisingly—and with the embarrassment, I might add, most usually attendant to such ill-apportioned and impossible wants—allowed yourself to seem, almost to act; should the telling of the tale in some way come to rule—or decidedly *affect*—the substance or the nature of that turning, then the moment of transition from account to mere performative will be signaled by a shift in the character of said terminus, or the telling of it as...

φ

Should it come to the fore that this very act of coming to the fore plays some...plays any role *at all* in the resumption of my purpose— the fulfillment of my ends, and so the promise to move on—then I would grant no quarter to those abstract insubordinates, an ideal that I have not yet pursued, or framed as cause. In the absence of a way to fully demonstrate my point, I'd justify its discharge by dint of the same instrument that's led me to accept the imposition of objections from the auditor, objections I've already raised myself. What I'm trying to say is...

φ

I expect you've found yourself beset by such chafing deportment many times before our meeting at this amicable stand, and so I ought not need continue my portrayal of the state I think you're more or less most suited to live *in*, but I've come to accept that supposition of the kind oft proves imprudent, which in this instance is more than likely equal to untrue. In this instance indicates the premise is untrue, and as such seems an impulse quite imprudent to engage...

φ

So how, you want to know, have I achieved this grand assize? To answer would amount to the confusion of my means with my ends, at least my ends with my beginnings. I suppose I'm only willing to suppose your acquiescence...I only here make *mention* of your willingness to suppose such wrenching suppliance *in me* at this first pass—this first pass *through*—in order to allay the damp of those for whom it seems a second nature, that they might come to tolerate the repetition of implicit terms...

φ

So. What I'm trying to say...to *prove* is that one can still rightly minimize—still *sacrifice*—the moment of confusion that's coerced this wayward turn, the moment that's confused *me* by compelling such contradictory ends. One need but think the guarantee by which I introduced myself mistaken—a fault that, understood as such, ought have no further impact on the this tittle of carousing goads...

φ

Merely to attest that what's to happen next—so far as it amounts to a performance of that happening by being self-identical with *fact*—is a description of the many failed attempts I've made at doing anything...anything *other* than attempt to describe my many failed attempts, whether any such attempt proves failed or not, would relieve the sort of reader I imagine *I* would be from further concern. It's only by beginning with an ending my beginning, in effect, still brings *about*—and by virtue of referring to some happenstance made real by the disclosure of a reference to that happenstance itself—that I've found reason to take issue with the primary this terminal incipience preempts...

φ

It isn't much to say that any scene made uninhabitable...made practically *unbearable* by a premise whose insistence trains a contrary resolve need but ask of its presumptive inculcator the extraction of said premise in order to continue on to more propitious ends, but I do not do so—I do not *say* so—because I think it less than obvious to those who've come to view it as an easy perch, a place to rest...

φ

And it may be thus—less than obvious, that is; it may well prove a tricky feint for those who've happened on it without previous and parallel pursuit. But *I* say it, alternately, because I can thereby ensure that those wise patrons still immured within my peerless and incorrigible brood will know I have not foisted said first premise falsely, without having concluded that within that premise something still left unresolved resides; that I am not as ill-equipped as any thinking otherwise—any thought that I've pressed on because I know no *better* than to do so—might reasonably suggest to all those listless mountebanks who have hearkened to the song...

φ

If one might grant the vision of this tell-all—of this *telling*, really, that what's been told therein may still amount to only part—as such a missive subornation, then I think the interlocutor to whom that missive points is halfway won. Her *sympathy*, that is, might be conditionally proved. And *this* point, rest assured, can only be rejected—let alone compelled into some promissory calm—by an equal adherence to contradictory ends; a registered receipt of what's been pledged as unreceivable, if for no other reason than its having not been mailed. If there are any so inclined, I'm happy to declare, they've surely put the book down long ago, before they started, and so I have no need to try to keep them in the fold...

φ

Halfway won, I say, the very state in which I found you, as you know with near certainty by now. I'm sure you don't conceive yourself as much further along in your attempts to train your quizzical departure into either an acceptance of the voyage still to greet you or—more likely—the contempt of one convinced to move along. Which is to claim...to here *admit* that I'm aware your being halfway *lost* has happened...*is happening* in answer to this salutary salvo, a practice I've adopted to promote such pained rapport...

φ

All the same, I won't predict that you'll accompany my soon to seem insufferable delays with anything but halfway measures—that your continuance amounts to...will *ever* amount to less than the acceptance of the intimacy of my discharge, as a missive intended for you alone. And even granting your adherence—witting or otherwise—to such contrived resolve, the pose is only possible if you're able to allow that I'm as...that I've *proved* myself just as aware of the iniquity—the contraindication by which I've sworn to make haste towards the prospect that this contrary portends as ready aim, as clear result...

φ

To summarize again, and this time for the first, this failed attempt plays precursor to all the many failed attempts it will soon serve to iterate...to *unconceal* to those who've found the strength to tag along. Attempts at what, I realize, you have yet to be enlightened; let it suffice to say that you will find out in due course...

φ

If it makes it any easier to accept the peculiarity of such unutterable self-reference, one might do well to notice that—while standing true as first—this failed attempt still claims it will succeed in its succession, and thereby will assume the equally exclusive posture of the last. Of my many failed attempts this may well be the first, but it is furthermore the *final*, and with any luck such character will wrest you from your wallow in this patchwork of a fundament—from *keeping pace* with what is soon to seem its sure collapse...

φ

And should this claim to certitude unwittingly deter some odd pur-veyor of the scene and its yet untold mise from keeping with me while I make my way from prelude to account, then I say good riddance. Someone's got to take the rubbish out, and convincing it to take *itself* is nothing less than a narrative coup. It seems just as unlikely that I'll ever gain the measure of that disaffected cohort, no matter how suc-cessfully I manage to do otherwise—to increase its pitch and flutter in the midst of such rebuke...

φ

A dwindling many or a countless few; a frenzied pullulation of devo-tional adherents or a supplicant's surrender to delirious decline; one need but to assume the possibility of it happening for it to scan as actual—so the claim that it's already happened *true*...

φ

Okay then. Let me start again. In the first place, let me start again. I'm sure you don't require an alleged reaffirmation of your willing-ness to continue to convince you of the wisdom of permitting me this...this *reprieve*, given what you've let me get away with to this point. If it indeed proves my intention to return to the beginning before I go too far in the continuance of my tale—and it does, let me assure you while I still maintain the gravitas to warrant such a vow—then the only thing to stop me, I can readily disclose, is my own damnable attachment to what I've done so far, and if some vain reversal were to vitiate that attachment, it would have done so prior to your ever having had the chance to browse...

φ

You can forthwith *assume* that this succeeding primary will remain just that—will remain *successive*—and so that my devotion to the parlor trick of etiquette is but one more way to vindicate an unrea-sonable...what one might rightly classify an *unreasoned* response. If it works, so be it; if not, then let me start another way, the way of starting out again I've only just begun to...

φ

Let me start again with something...I don't know...something more *vernacular*, if not precisely common to the argot broadly sanctioned as the acme of locutionary verve. Let me start the scene again; it hardly seems the first instance of such disjunctive posturing to rate the marginalia of the empty page...

φ

I awoke that day with little...nay, with *nothing* on my mind—a quietude most usually thought evidence of contentment, although it's oft coincident with other feeling modes. And while such vague affinity may impute the subtle ornament of causation to some distended prelude or remorseless fugue, it was not so on the day in question, the day with which...whose first moments of consciousness I've chosen to begin with...to begin *again* with, admitting even *this* attempt at telling holds the prospect of beginning for a *second* second time...

φ

To begin with that same cognizance of drifting off that I'd have sensed had I been at the moment of the drifting made content by some condition or collation of conditions in...in what would have to be...to be *and* seem my present state—the state in which that scene transpired presently, and not the present state of its recall...

φ

The sense that I awoke to, I became at once aware, was suggestive of contentments I'd awoken in before, but this presumed diversion...this *insistence*, as it were, had been neither occasioned by a circumstance

I'd judged to be desirable—let alone desired—nor by expectation of some circumstance to come. I was merely there, trapped in an unrelenting clarity with nothing to see clearly and no target to divert me from those same discrepant ends, other than the breaking of the trance that any notice brought to bear upon a scene is sure to cause. It was as though an absence...as though I'd *come upon* an absence, a bound beyond which there was nothing left to fate or chance—to stimulate awareness of such stimulus *or* response...

φ

I found myself corralled within that feckless grace—that *startled fluency*—no dream to break the silence, no wisp of cloud to blot my view of sky. And despite this novel...this *newfound* ataraxia—or without consideration of it any way at all—I began my day as I always had, moiling in the bed clothes till I'd marked the addled maunder of some portion of my figure into shadow, a process just as likely to take half the day as some mere instant to occur...

φ

The measure of the passage of some collop into umbra—some part or part of part that *had* been blighted by the day—depends on both the locus of one's preceding arousal and the attitude of desiccated corpus likewise ciphered...

φ

It is not my way to tarry, I should confess, but neither will I rush through those scant signposts that could serve to set me straight along my righteous course. No good can come of it, as far as I'm concerned, although this claim suggests I've reaped the lessons of that haste, when my only recollection of an instance of said learning...when I have no recollection of an instance of said learning—of an instance of the sort that I've learned *from*—only boundless recollections of similarly referencing the lessons of imaginary pratfalls...

φ

I'm not always in the same place, a mere moment's recollection of so many moments past makes perfectly clear. My memory of those instances in which I'd been reminded that I ought not leave without my wan ablutions...without the rigid practice of *perceptual* ablution by which I greet each coming day puts that froward regimen in whereabouts that may appear distinct—read as *distinguishable*—despite the fact that many are repeated...

φ

If there are only one or two that bear repeating—that are manifestly echoed in the bearing of the vestiges they trail—then I feel confident in my belief that some more formal repetition may satisfy the presently pursuant...the demonstrable *pursuit* of that one present in particular, when I awoke to recollect that some imperiled clarity would only cede into an active tense after I had let that static luminance reveal...*concoct* the derivations thus redacted as discerned...

φ

I know what you're thinking. You're thinking...

φ

First, I think you're thinking that I can't know what you're thinking; that what you're thinking *now* is but one of many things you *could* be thinking, given the divulgence of so little over so much time. You're thinking that you don't know where to start with your objections to such dithering abstraction in the *absence* of all predicates—an absence by which you are here advertently engaged; *how* to next proceed with your aspiring objections to the many unexplained—in some way *inexplicable*—details that evoke a paltry inkling of the scene...

φ

Should anyone, that is to say—that one that you amount to, that you've more or less accepted as the sum of those adventures most responsible for tempting you to lend me your concern...

φ

Should anyone *take issue* with the nature of my project, not merely for indulging this intrepid peroration, but equally for its placement just beside the point of planning it—the planning that remains beside the point the plan entails—then why continue on with the objection *or* its answer? Why bother bothering to uncover the point that there's no point to what's *essentially* beside the point, always as the point beside the point the side contrives? Why complain of points one has since understood as pointless—as having no relation to some broader scope or scale—when it's not even clear that such a scope is in the offing, or if it is that it *will* be for long enough to mark it and take aim? Why, indeed, when one can simply bound off to the coda, to skim those trifling bits that might inspire some new steel? Go ahead, then. I'll wait. I have no place else to go. And if, alas, you don't return, then let this vow of patience prove the fondest of farewells...

φ

Steven Seidenberg

φ

You're back. Satisfied? I can't imagine. I can't, that is, imagine that you found what I imagined you were looking for when—or *if*—you took the time to look for...You've made the choice to start again with this...this *intermediary* genesis, and by so doing have accepted the impending range of what's herein implied—or its' absence, even; whatever were the grounds of your demurrer when we parted ways...

φ

I attest to thee, my friend, if you could but take a view of my head— or at least the bloated foretop that embellishes its pale—then alas, let me tell you, 'tis so bruised and misshaped with the blows that your compatriots have given me in the dark, that should I recover, and mitres thereupon be suffered to rain down from heaven as thick as hail, not a one of them would fit it...

φ

And if you're one of those who didn't take my offer—as though you'd need permission to do just as you will—then it's probable you'd made your choice preceding my admonishment, and all this going on about first order objections has never once applied to you, or your reproof. Maybe you'll find whimsy—or solace, better still—in knowing that when such discordance rises to *your* sightline there's a chance—the slightest chance—that I'll address it in good time, all in good time. Which is more than I can say for what's most usually vouchsafed as the apex of the literary stock and trade...

φ

For now, I will assume that you have overcome what troubled you when I first brought your notice to the exits on this stage—a comfort in your presence, I would humbly remind you, I have made no strides against, or claims upon. I'm *comforted,* that is to say, in knowing that you've put yourself at ease without assistance, that should you find yourself disturbed in future course you'll know you could do otherwise—could give up giving yourself up to it—and so that your continuance still constitutes a choice. Mine too, but that's beside the point...

φ

Which brings me to the trouble I believe I know you're troubled by—the sort I gather vexes those in league with this account. There are, I am aware, still many possible objections to specific turns within what I've discovered to this point; they may in fact be *countless,* lo these many inclinations to take issue with a turn of phrase, a metaphor, a gest—any passage one can call a principle, or an inference...

φ

They may be countless, I'll admit, but such avowal yields too little margin to be of any use—or too much, one could say, with the identical results...

φ

I said I knew your thinking, but now I'm not so sure—of either what you're thinking now or what you were when I first made the claim. I guess I meant to say...no, I said what I meant; I thought I knew your thoughts—and I may have, it remains unclear...remains *for me* to clarify. That you need think no further on the matter goes without saying...without saying or thinking, I should say, or think...Whether I knew what you were thinking or not, I meant to say I thought I did—I'm saying now I thought I did, which is evidenced by having said so then...

φ

The *truth* of an assertion, after all is said and done, has little to do with the intent of its maker—with what is thus meant *by* it—a truism I'd like to grant as though proved somewhere else. But that's not right. It's a premise, I believe, of some considerable import, if not precisely yet, then in some circumstance to come. I feel confident—*I state it as a truth*—that sooner or later having given further evidence...further *explanation* for this generalized conjecture will prove proof of something *else*—something that's not even thought incipient at present—and it seems to me such confidence is more than worth the effort of some casual pursuit...

φ

Let us, as a model, say this claim to future value—of the value of some similar assertion in a world to come—proves mistaken or a waste of time, at minimum provides no evidence to the contrary. That I was wrong—even that my being wrong should beckon me to postulate some providential sooth—doesn't mean that I meant something other than the claim thereby precluded, or disproved. What I mean to say, I mean to say, when I say I mean otherwise—or what I *meant* to when I did so, at *this* unyielding turn, accepting that the same plaint may apply in future course...

φ

What I was meaning to *divulge* was what first led me to the claim I've since refuted—that I knew what you were thinking when it turns out I knew nothing of the sort. Maybe not nothing—maybe *of the sort*, at least—at least in that my thoughts on what you are or have been thinking *might* have been the case, when I couldn't yet have *known* any such thing...

φ

I haven't said just what that was, I'll grant you, assuming that the absence of my saying—and consequently of your knowing—was what you were just thinking of just now. My point is that *whatever* I first thought that you were thinking could not have been in all cases *born out*, as any set described as such—as means to *aggregate* that lot—must be construed indefinite in scope, meaning no one league of arbiters—such as we are, one assumes—can conceivably have covered its full breadth. I *may* have been correct in the conjecture, to clarify the point, but I couldn't then have *known* I was, and as I said I did I can now claim with *perfect* certainty—can know, as proven *fact*—that I was wrong...

φ

What does it really mean, then, for me to have meant otherwise—to have meant *to say* otherwise? I know forsooth I didn't, and that you have no reason to believe I thought I did when I first claimed. What I should have said...what I *meant* to say when I said I meant something...something other than I *did* mean, at *that* peculiar stand, was that my deft mistake, now that I realize that I made it, comes with an explanation of precisely where—and by what means—my meaning went awry...

φ

What I was doing...what I meant to show...what was *shown up* by my...my *inclination* to believe that you'd do just as I would if presented with the same prodigious positure, as you have been—as we have *both* been, it appears, however many pairings we contrive ourselves to form—hoping, all the while, that you'd *more* than do as I did...as I *have* by sovereign testament of doing so; that more than merely doing so you'd *think* so—that your doing so would follow... would *have followed* the same circuit I, too, have done...

φ

I, too, have raised objections to the measure of my circumstance against so many instances of similar repose, and knowing myself quite well I'm able to reveal...to *unconceal*, I say again, the motive and the reason behind doing so, that it should meet the standard of its placement in this tale. This précis to—or *of*—what will soon come to seem a tale...

φ

I mean to say I understand that you might not have access to the same muddle of reasoning that's led me to my...my what, I'm still unsure, but regardless that in *this* way you can't cogitate as I do—or haven't yet sustained such course for more than the mere instant of objecting to its practice here and now. I want...I *wanted* to believe that the objection I was making, though unspoken, was still shared—having like minds, as I've always hoped we would...perchance we do—but there are differences between us...between my lone proximity to this parody of prosy vim and yours, differences that guarantee your reading is still partial...is always *less* complete than mine is, an assertion that I'd think you'd have no trouble thinking true...

φ

Take the claim as flattery or insult, whatever suits your mood, but even thus accepting some like affect in receipt of this odd gibe the asymmetry of our relation to its lexical purlieus—to all that is meant by this general affect of a broader view—is mirrored in its obverse, as a limit on the voicing of a future plan. *I*, that is to say, do not have access to *your* locus in relation to this colloquy—*your* scansion and *your* path—and so you are as likely to hit on some new insight—some tremble that remains a novel variance to me. As likely as I am. And while we both may stub our toes on some one fissure in the pavement, there are surely many others I've alone avoided in my parallel resumption of a parallel decline...

φ

Too bad, really. I'd like to have heard your musings on the matter—on what the matter *is*, if not an aid to its discharge. I'd like the chance to glean your chance rebuttal to this missive, or understand such schism as the dereliction of the scene to come. Haven't we all felt it? The hateful deformity of the endeavor—the *exertion*—of throwing one's insipid elocutions off the summit, believing someday something will return...

φ

I'm not trying to prefer this as some new form of indemnity; don't take me for a fool, it will do neither of us good. Or both of us harm. More harm than the mere absence of some good. I know as well as anyone that I've given myself over to indomitable usury—that I will never get back what I'm due, what I deserve. This perseveration is expenditure, it's true, but it has been enacted for the sake of such expenditure alone; a potlatch that, with any luck, will leave my coffers empty when it's done...

φ

It is *at least* assured that the conceit of this remembrance—this memento of an age that's passing by as it's recalled—is that there's someone...some *many* who are hardly of a different mind than I am here and now but for the incidental contours of propinquity, of being not right here right now as I am, I suppose. I Suppose *you're* not, but I would rather it were otherwise, that we could still believe we walked together...

φ

Such pretense aside...put *beside* consideration, which is not strictly out of...out of reach, beyond regard, I can...I *did* take the position that you were placed as I am; that *if* you were, I'd know...I *would have known* your thinking, what you were thinking *of* when I first made the claim...

φ

I thought I ought inform you I had realized—in the event you've had the good fortune of realizing it too—that I had offered some-thing...some attempt at explanation that required explanation in its own right, if not in the end then surely when considered as a measure of the short view...

φ

How, if you were thinking it—thinking of the same *it* in its turn—can I suggest the distance between moments of repose by thus recall-ing them with that in mind—for the sole and sidelong purpose of evoking such singular ends? I feel no obligation to provide you with an answer...to *accept* the query now, before its censure or delay, and so you may take up my taking up of what you likely first conceived as your concern alone with trepidation, with a wary sensitivity that's sure to serve you well...

φ

Perhaps I ought to here confess my fondness for redundancy, even though I'm not sure if it's yet come into view; once again I tell you that, although this last *perhaps* may seem more tactic than disposi-tive, I've never much concerned myself with planning my next step—with where and when, that is to say, my next step will hit ground.

The shortest path between *two* points may well be straightaway, but multiply the number of such nodes along one's course and one might *most* effectively take a route that stands to hit a few. As if the least expenditure in reaching our release is the conditional that sets us to our bearing, our *pursuit*...

φ

What I *seemed* to claim, it seems to me, to such giddy effect was that my recollections of said moments passing—moments much like those with which my tale...some *portion* of my tale begins to come about—were similar with respect to the concern that brought me to them—that brought my *notice* to them, if nothing more or else—but still appear distinct in ways I can't seem to state clearly...to describe with any clarity, and so make clear *to you*...

φ

It's not that it's so difficult to *imagine*, as I see it—as I imagine it, I might as well admit—but despite that ease I have not fairly winnowed down the options—have not chosen any one or two or three...not *picked* a single one, that is, to justify the boast. To make it represent some wayward *something* in particular, or some *things*, as I've since confessed to knowing is the more accurate account, and I'm convinced that if *I* were the one thereby forbidden proper access to the setting of the scene I might soon find my puzzlement transfigured into animus, or easy mirth...

φ

Needless to say, I am not bidden *or* forbidden to avail myself of such acquaintanceship, but I have my sympathies—a fact that I will surely need remind you of again. If I expect to make my way along the course of my odd coursings—or expect *you*, that is, not merely to take me at my word but to take my word the way *I* would if I were in *your* place—then I count it in my interest—an *obligation*, really, whether it proves in my interest or not—to provide you with a mode of understanding that will yield us *both* novel results...

φ

As such, let me tell you, no one set of many moments I can presently recall has revealed anything but the practice of awakening as precedent to that peculiar feeling—peculiar to you, it seems to me, to any one of you—with which the day in question...that one day *in particular* began...

φ

No precedence can vindicate my choosing *not* to throw myself out of repose and into...into whatever I've found myself reposing in—perhaps upon—when I've been thrown out into...can *gird* my choice to bide within such immotile posture until finding my place again within that obtuse frame, nor can I recall a single circumstance to warn me of the dangers of proceeding before coming to that clarity of purpose and impression, that finally elucidated mise-en-scene...

φ

This, it seems to me, is strange enough. But stranger still, I think, what I've been forced to recollect as something to recall before I further limn what stopped me from all furthering along is that within my summing up of instances the same—the same for having thus discerned no consequence...no single *undesired* consequence to dodging such routine—I claimed certain disparities between those disparate instances, differences I've yet to name, or press into the service of...of anything one can construe an absence, or a squandered gain...

φ

There was a time when I awoke not knowing what I woke to, or where I had set down the night before. I've often found it true that

the exception proves revealing on occasions when an endless iteration
of the rule can never do, a truism I'm sure you'll take no issue with...
Well, I'm not precisely sure, but let us say, for lack of a more friendly
confirmation, that in this instance—if no other—I don't care...

φ

There was a time some time ago when I awoke in calm and carefree
humor, without a sense of where I was or was, in turn, *moved towards*, but even at that moment I was more or less accustomed to
the habits I have subsequently come to grant as commonplace...as
commonplace *to me,* in present rank and form, a search for hint of
shadow slung across the fading view...

φ

I *say* search, but that's not what I was doing...what I *thought* that I
was doing at the time. In retrospect, I understand the impulse as the
flailing of a child in the first throes of its métier, without the slightest
whisper of such forthcoming accord...

φ

I imagine there are many who would find this disconcerting—a sudden apprehension of the generally impalpable complexion of prevenient pursuit. It's routine to credit feats of artistry or ratiocination as
the coming to fruition of some crop sown in the womb, but the incidental contours of one's unwitting propinquity are just as wholly *of
oneself,* as rightly thought *authentis*; still constitute the prowess we've
indentured ourselves *to...*

φ

And why not. Or what other choice. The question, it appears to me,
has nothing at all to do with the act in...in *question*, I'm inclined to
say, despite my realization that such desultory diction might prove

counter to my fealty to the phrase *well-turned*; my *awareness* that the saying of it thusly might impress the churlish quidnunc as divergence from my customary weal...

φ

There is nothing one can do that one can't equally invest with so much value that it looms above all other patent aims—all other *doings*, if my meaning is unclear; nothing that one can't at least conceive of standing out as unexampled, as the zenith of what constitutes such value as an end. It's exactly this investment that leads most men to their leanings, if they should be among the privileged few who get the choice, and if they're merely tossed into some fitful avocation, such investiture may lead them to a vision of its betterment, its perfect—or *perfected*—course...

φ

I recall the flitting entry of the light into my eyes, the opening of the world that seems the first blush of the day. That the first blush of the daylight seems. I recall that first unknowing, if you'll permit the term, the search for some belonging, some acquaintance with the view, and so for what one might call place in what one might call world...

φ

This is how one comes to think a circumstance familiar, as *of a kind* with somewhere one has been before; one feels one's humble locus as relation, not as feature; as though one's sense of being set within it marks the limits of the portent thus redacted as indelible, as *sure*...

φ

I have my place, I think, or so I've frequently professed; I have a place in this world that in that one I'm without, a place of ease or tension I'm excluded from in other...in what can't help but seem to me as *other* disparate worlds for the construction of that compass by the subject set within it...beyond it...against it...whatever sense that subject has of *its* place in the scene. As though the set of things and attributes of things construed as ground could ever *make room* for such placement or abjure the very same, despite its being equal to the idling composite that it has been or it will be just a moment hence...

φ

Is there really any reason to belabor the point? Can it *possibly* remain obscure, my considerable difficulty in divulging it notwithstanding? I don't know, in answer to your...to *my* question, really, a question that I once again—and for the same reasons—attribute to the second that I'm eager to assume—and this for reasons *un*-disclosed—will take its answer in. I won't dwell on it; whether you *would* have asked the question had I failed to ask it for you is of no real...no *measureable* consequence, at least not once it's proffered, once it's *posed*...

φ

I don't know, I repeat—and likewise in response to the inquiry I'd like to think we share in this regard—whether I've expressed to anyone what troubles me; what makes it *worth* the trouble to describe at such great length what we have all...what *most* of us have taken to—have granted and made use of—in traversing this milieu, so far as it's sustained. As though one could sustain a thing—could think it as *enduring*—without that thing extended, or extending...

φ

More interesting, perhaps, is that I'm able to use metaphors of magnitude—of *relative* magnitude—that make no extrinsic reference, that only have a *bearing* in the midst of this parole. I *merely* claimed, in case you missed it, that I'd begun to perorate at such great length on details greatly piled up by virtue of my claiming them; that the measure of the former has exceeded...is in the *process* of exceeding the latter, and that this act of overage is expressly what I should *not* do—what shouldn't have made sense...made sense of making sense, that is, impelled as such or no...

φ

It would seem a simple reflex—it would prove *unproblematic*—if one were to say...to similarly *compare* the extent to which a thing is limned with that of...of some gathering of predicates belonging to what's been described already with less interest or resolve...

φ

The construal of some alter with the same set as its object—the object one is patently attempting to construe—might not be *most* effective, but in principle ought work as well as any other mode...

φ

How compare the length of a description with the greatness of detail that makes it up? How measure the time it takes to do a thing against the assiduity...the *absurd* assiduity of one's efforts towards achieving that ingenuous design—the completion of one's vision of a better world, or one's unstinting failure to effect such change...

φ

It is possible, one must assume, to go on at great length and have that length appear a lesser when compared to some still greater pass, or for some monstrous aggregate of predicable particulars to pale in comparison to another deposition of the same. This is just to recapitulate what seems to me self-evident—that insofar as something's quantifiable there's always an imaginable greater than and lesser to that rule, conceding that it may still seem the greatest or the least that one has come upon...has *yet come* to conceive. So one can have gone on at great length in one's attempts to limn in great or minor detail, but such is neither lesser to nor greater than the quantum of detail therein declaimed, for having no one scale on which to measure both...

φ

The figure works in *some* way, nevertheless; it is *not*, that is, nonsensical, despite the inconsistency of the claim it rests upon. The affinity, as I see it—as it now appears I *meant* it, though I still can't say for sure—is not between the length of the digression and the superfluity of its sum, but the state of ease or anger in the subject who receives it—to whom such nearly deafening excursus is declaimed. If one somehow diverges from what's thought one's *proper* path—the path of least resistance in fulfillment of one's wants—then both the novel passage and the method to traverse it are factors in the measure of resultant stress...

φ

It may be true that limping over sodden hill or lumpen sprawl will take less time than any breathless flight around the world, but to limp around the world...

φ

The scene that I awoke to was directly unfamiliar, which suggests, it seems to me, that I had not been there before—that having at the ready no clear notion of so being, I might presume that I had never hitherto been so...

φ

And I'm willing to go further; if one wakes in a strange room, discerning that the place of such arousal *is* a room—a sort of *habitation*, of *any* shape or span—then one may be decided it's familiar in its kind;

and if within one's field of view one finds evidence of prostration—a manger or a pallet or perhaps even a bed—then one feels in a setting, a context that's contrived to bring about familiar ends...

φ

But if one can't discern a single nuance of inclusion, of where one is and with what discrete objects one's arrayed, if nothing about anything portends a use or function, or seems to be construed with any final cause in mind, then the sense of perturbation—of bewilderment and rage—is of another order, a sort I'd like to claim I was immured in when...

φ

In retrospect it seems that I awoke just as I have both fore and aft this subject of...the subject of *this instance* of recall, the final iteration in that series coming...*having come upon me* this very day. This day that I now voice within, now that I voice within it, as though I might make haste towards its compulsory completion before a next arousal should alight upon...

φ

But such concern must wait another time—perhaps another *life*—to be addressed. Let us take as our position—as our *premise*, better yet—that although I have awoken many times before and since, that day that I refer to as the first I was immersed in such pervasive incoherence—a generalized discomfiture I've only just *suggested*, let alone impelled to suffer through the privilege of account—is expressly the right place for me to restart this compendium, and so for reasons only clear should I soon manage...*have the strength* to travel forward...

φ

If I had failed to ascertain the practice that would lead me to...to all the rest that's crossed my path while slowing this career, I'm not sure I could even have described it as an absence, a privation, as it were, of any stable sort at all. If, that is, I had not *sallied forth* from that confusion, I don't believe I'd ever have had any sense of what it was or where I was within it, let alone have claimed it as the portent of some realm to come; I would not find it knowable as prescient—as *predictive*—so everything that followed it would need remain unknown...

φ

*To be familiar* is not to contrive one's chosen object—the object that one thus purports to be familiar *with*—as separate from the state in which it no less seems to happen, but also to have recognized...to have cognized *again* the *type* of place it's placed in, fit to frame and core by all its constituted parts. All of its constituents, so every singularity one classifies as in. I tell you this—or think this *through* with you in such an intimate proximity—in order to suggest the very minimum discernment of what otherwise would never have been offered as...*appended to* the tyranny of the real...

φ

Scope a common lane that one has never before travelled and one might have some difficulty taking in the view, but one is still content to think that one is on a byway, upright and directed towards some unknown turn. Such a newfound aspect is still fixed in known relation—relation to whatever one's relating to, that is—but what one deems familiar hardly constitutes a knowledge of its conflicts and conformities, one's sense of having come upon a world both whole and new...

φ

One may have no idea what force impels passing conveyances—conveyances that travel on to distant, hidden ends; no notion what decisive stroke bereaved the path of dangers, or how the buildings rise up without geologic goads; one has always inured oneself to living in an outline, to striding in and through a world *essentially* unseen—a world that may be understood essentially *unseeable*, for having neither medium nor method to see more...

φ

And even if one *has* such skill one may not want to use it—one may be fully satisfied with one's received engagement with that circumstance one thinks to thereby bracket as one's own, and so be glad to presently forgo unanswered questions, to leave them to a time when they will scan as either exigent or profitable...

φ

Which claim reveals the next point of significant distinction from the general understanding of the terms in my employ—another node of unfamiliarity with what a proper picture of the present scene demands. So I'd like to *emphasize* your singular position in relation to the strangeness I began this missive *in*; that you are unfamiliar with the variant of unfamiliarity I'm trying here to explicate, as I was till I found myself imprisoned...

φ

And let me reassure you, if you'll permit the pose—it was not witting. I'm not *certain*, I should say, that it will serve you as a comfort; that anything I do can contravene the sense you have...the sense I take no umbrage in accepting you've *adopted* that your efforts have been squandered, if not purposely misused. That *I* am wasting *your* time with such hoo-hah and deflection, even as its object...as its *value* should seem so discretely poised...

φ

My aim is not to coax you to a sympathetic interlude with my pecu-

37

liar interludes—my more or less intransigent imbroglio of ends; if you're lost to me by now then you would never reach the good parts...you would surely be incapable of coming to the good parts and knowing that you'd...that you'd merely *done* so—that you'd come up upon them as they litter your advance...

φ

I thought you might *appreciate* that I've been just as viciously abandoned to this mire of impertinent defenses and congenial rebuffs; that you might feel less able...less *eager* to accredit the opprobrium that's welling in the narrows of your system should you realize that I, too, would be unwilling to go down this road had it been set before me as a plan...

φ

Alas, this was not my fate, which doesn't prove I don't know what I'm doing; I don't want to *give you any ideas*, as it were. I guess it proves I don't know *everything* I'm doing, insofar as such a boundless set most certainly—and most *importantly*—need include all those affairs preceding present circumstance—all circumstance of unequal *or* similar significance...and so on. I take this vow not, as you might suspect, because my modesty has overwhelmed the pressing flow of lucubrations; not with any generosity of spirit and regard, but to reassure you that the *contrary* is definitively untrue; that although I don't confess from some propulsive sense of penitence, neither do I go on like this—like *this* this that I'm on about right now—for the arrogance of an ill-will or a callous wit...

φ

I don't know everything I'm doing, to continue the point, as demonstrated by what I'm doing as I'm saying that I don't know what I'm doing to continue doing something that I *thought* that I was doing—something other than what I first *said* I thought I was...

38

I thought I *would*...

φ

Actions have consequences, as we are all plainly aware; everything that happens recapitulates some happening before. Everyone has lived the rule of unintended consequences—that no one can take stock of every influence one's actions have beyond one's general view. Yes, yes, you say, what of it; you are compelling in your reasoning, but *I* still know everything *I'm* doing as it intersects with that one world I was approaching when...

φ

You, rather. I want to say that *you* were saying I, and so was not referring to the I that I've surrendered as a speaker to this point—this present that I point to, that I've discerned I'm pointing to by pointing thus at all. This may also have been perfectly clear. If only I believed you'd meet your *next* assured confusion with a similar ease of mind then I'd be well positioned to avoid such crude redundancy in future course, but as you don't appear to be so charitably inclined...

φ

It's perfectly clear to everyone that results often diverge from one's prevenient intents—intents that first advanced one's sense of purpose as inceptive, if nonetheless still subject to delayed remove. This is not to say such ends are always undesirable, merely undesired—as likely to be seen as a fortuitous surprise as the thwarting of a plan. Well, not *as* likely, but enough to make such glad receipt seem unremarkable—hardly worth the effort of remarking...

φ

I don't know why I need all this...this *justification*, when any premise to the contrary seems not only stupid but absurd. Again one may attribute to the nature of one's actions—particularly to those of such symbolic kind—the easily admonished inner carriage of a will that's only manifest in subsequence, but that does little...*nothing*, really, to assuage the waiting pique of those who fancy the determinant of autonomous causation at work in every flinch and twinge. Every impulse that presents itself as primary...

φ

Accept, then, my apologies for having to divert you in the name of some remediation whose continuance, on second thought, we both might well be better off without. It's not to say—it *never* is—that I've forged some new contract, or have as my intention to do other else again—when presently we find ourselves within the *next* diversion, however it should pass into the present frame. It would be a sure mistake for me to here make promises I may know that I *can* keep but that I'm not certain I *want* to, believing all my efforts on the way to such fulfillment would result in greater loss, but I can guarantee you this; you can take me at my word when I affect such dreary apologue, a lesson you'd do well to mind when it comes round again...

φ

If nothing else, it seems I've brought us forward to this station—it seems to me this station is some distance from the port where we set sail. There is, I think we've shown—or I've adduced with your assistance, granting that it may be only grudgingly bestowed—something that connects one's basic ease within one's circumstance—an ease that may well prove undue a moment past or hence—with that sense of estrangement that most challenged my contentment when this inchoate codicil *cast off*...

φ

The claim is indisputable, at least once it's been made; in order for some incident to seem, as such, familiar—to *be* familiar, rather, in its proper place and time—it must already be surveyed within familiar precincts, beyond which...well, beyond which one can't think of, let alone discern...

φ

The face, then, of the newly minted subject of one's glower, though often unfamiliar to the one thereby enthralled, is nonetheless set off against familiar pulse and purview, but let that selfsame personage vociferate in unknown tongue and soon it drifts so far from what *appeared* its steadfast nature it's not even understood as being fit to the same form. One can repeat the exercise in fact as well as mind—and with any sort of target, whether inert or alive—and mark my words, one's sense of living in familiar borders will first shift with the tenor of the batten and the backdrop, *then* in some accordance with the thing presumed within it...that might have moved within it, surging from the coulisse to the stage...

φ

All this to prepare the scene—by helping inculcate a sense of what the preparation of the scene requires, so delays. What the absence of that preparation proves—or *would* have proved had I been guilty of it...of *eliding* such exordial demands—is what you must be first familiar with if you're to soon approach...to know that it's the scene *you are approaching*...

φ

The scene that you're approaching is perceived as worth the effort that the enterprise of such approach indelibly prolongs by its apparent unfamiliarity to that hapless deviser who seems to be so unfamiliar with its varied terms, and thus I have indulged the prolix paradox of making you familiar with the unfamiliar pitch that rose to meet me when I woke, on that first day...

φ

If you understand my purpose then you'll have no further trouble with the claim that my description of the scene is incomplete. Will remain, that is, incomplete. I can't have been the first to come across this odd vexation, the insistence of a memoir that commences with such bafflement—an indeterminable deficit of determinable events. What, in the end, can mark an absence one can't think an absence *from*? How, in the vernacular, is the want of common standard to be taken for a standard? How make a rule of having no more rules...

φ

But I've surged too far ahead of the point. Too far ahead of the behind whose seeming aftermath we scan. As though one could accuse me of an undue passing over of particulars proved central to some plot to come. As though there were a plot to come, or you could *know* there were a plot to come...

φ

It's a relative measure, after all; the speed of passing quarry is gauged only in relation to the speed at which the salvo that its passing moves, and each is only made out in distinction from that stillness which serves *all* movement as ground...

φ

If I've given you a glimpse of the fate that will befall me—what was but what has yet to be betrayed as having been—then you'll accept my once and future failure to invoke the fretful passage I've ostensibly begun this emprise with. Or in. Within which I've begun to claim—if not outright *confess*—that there may still be something like a proof of my achievement in this derelict regard but only *you* can make it, as I'm in no position to adjudge your understanding of my objects, so my ends. I'll leave it to you; if you've ascertained the substance and the purview of my purpose then you'll have no trouble making it suffice. And if you have begun to think I bode *no* steady course, then you're really coming round to my predicament; the challenge is to generalize such vagrancy to the world at large...

φ

Absence is only failure if some fill remains one's goal. The claim is tautological, and only needs be offered to be presumed a truth by those who've been conferred the gift of making claims at all. I can't say that you're one of them, but *I* was when the first hint of that absence hit my eye—the absence of all sense of the familiar, I remind you, of what such brazen cognizance might look like in relation to an absence rightly understood as found...

φ

It's why the moment appears singular, at least in my recall. I'd awoken many times without a sense of where I was—or where I had laid down, that is, the night or week before—but always before *that* time I'd been able to find something...some common stance or object within proximate regard—a *usual* from which to build a bounding sense of agency...a sense of bounding agency, if not at once a life *properly formed*...

φ

Perhaps an example would be useful—would help to bring the paradox of posture without purchase into view. Let me think. Not you, I know; I don't need *your* permission. I will long since have done what I've asked you to *let* me by the time you've had your sneer. These things are not transparent; what's routinely understood as some mere nuance of rhetorical practice is made significant by a mechanism interior to the colloquy itself, and while I know the trope will work without further analysis, there are times when such examination proves profitable in its own right, if for no other reason than assembling a system both consistent and complete without an outside...without *referring* to an outside...

♀

I'm not trying to suggest there aren't others...that I have reason *to believe* there aren't others equally dispirited by such probative delays, but neither do I need affirm the counter proposition to presume your supplication to my roving axiology, a pose one might think easier, if not *at one's ease*. This may not be true for you or your muling compatriots; you may find yourself a cohort who would rather shout aggrievements than abide the giddy succor of some self-correcting muse, but in this instance I'm happy to encourage your attrition; I tell you now beforehand, before your *next* debouch, put the book down at once. For you will no more penetrate the moral of the next marbled page than the world with all its sagacity has been able to unravel the many opinions, transactions and truths which still lie mystically hid under the dark veil of the black ones...

♀

And what's the harm in that? Well, it's not so much the harm as the privation of advantage, advantage that might otherwise be readily secured. Once again, an *absence* proves occasion for my insight, suggesting for the first time what it seems I now expect you to expect of such an influx of...of *not* lux, I think it's fair to say...

♀

It is commonly assumed that any absence wants filling, and perhaps it is most commonly the case, but such a filling may not be consistent with one's purpose, either at the present turn or what will come to seem one's proper state. One loses what there is to gain by *not* filling the absence when one fills it, it seems reasonable to suggest, thus the value of the practice first contrasts the absence filled with the absence made

by filling it, and some small deviation from one's mustering of focus—that it rouses the frustration of the speaker or the one thereby
made witness—surely isn't adequate to quash the generous profit
such excursus stands to harvest, as a matchless yield...

φ

So. An example. I'm trying to think of an example—something that
I've forced myself to do by forcing you to let me do it. For this, if
nothing else, let me express my gratitude—perhaps you'll even have
the chance to *exercise* the choice...

φ

Being *compelled* to do something doesn't make one's doing it any less
an act of kindness, even courage. No option *but* continuance isn't
proof one wouldn't have continued otherwise, and having been ac-
corded such a personal dispensation, the attitude one takes in doing
what one must do is all that differentiates fulfillment of one's duty
from the same act against interest absent secondary prod. One may
have been impressed into the battle as it rages, but one still chooses
one's comportment in responding to the call...

φ

In attempting to exemplify such discrete exemplification I've determined that the gest could only ever go for naught—that it could never properly communicate the sense I'm going after, or after which,
that is to say, I'm trying to proceed. I awoke within a hebetude unlike any I'd experienced before, a fact I was aware of at the moment
that I did so, not in least part for my dithering attempts to grasp
for something...to do anything...my *simultaneous* and immediately
*failed* attempts to find any sort of basis for the doing and the grasping
still to come...

φ

And that's explicitly my fear—or my reasoning, I should say; that in the course of such narration—such as *this* supernal din—everything is thought to function properly in *some* way, for the discretion of the author in avoiding its excise. In the excise of whatever odd attempts at demonstration I've since made on your behalf, I've since assumed that such attempts will go for naught for having naught to go…

φ

Having had a proper think about the use of the example in the service of narrating those events that are…that are elsewise *unexampled*, I have at least a notion that describing what has never been…what's never had a context or a distance to belong to—conceived as any set convened by attribute or cause—might be best accomplished in a manner that won't pledge the canny reader to the burden of cajoling its rewards…

φ

I have no way to represent that strangely pivotal impassivity, as all such ways appear to be beyond my present troth…and so it goes. It is, you may have gathered, a regression that at bottom grounds the simplest narration of the simplest details—established by the claim that signifying only happens after something is accepted as significant; after something acts as reference—as some *inertial* reference—for the symbol that the symbol that's in motion stands to yield…

φ

Which is only to declare that, while my very first awakening—awakening to what would send me down *this* errant trail—was not as any had been, nor as any has been since, it was still apprehended by the potentate now speaking—in whose lurid strain of reportage the milieu thus attended first commenced. By me, that is. The me that I would be if I were other…

φ

It was not without precedent, if in this regard alone; I was still the I that lived as I until that moment, and thereby served as reference for all future change in view. It ought to be accepted that the suppliance I've fostered as the cipher of a speaker—as the voicing of a world in which I've found myself a part—is still the same I I was then, at what's *since* then become the very cradle of my story, just as then I was the same I I had been *up to* then...

φ

I will not argue further the necessity of thinking of the person that I'm thinking of as singularly placed, as though I've had...I've ever had a chance to...I can at least *begin* with the encompassing absentia that I found so disconcerting, despite what might have otherwise been taken for delight, by bringing out the fullness in which those inclined to follow are intrinsically confined as they surrender to the margins—to the straightened line, I say, *and to the bent*...

φ

I'm in it too, I suppose—insofar as I'm still able to recall being outside it for a time. Even at that moment that I *can't* conjure an image of, I'm able to imagine for you something like the state of mind that finding no clear image of that moment left me in—the same that *you* might hold pressed into similar assessment, if not precisely similar display. Not that you have been, of course, but it's this that keeps you reading—or has, I feel convinced, up to this point; the fact that you have yet to live the spectrum of that species, even *conceived* of such congestion or its absence...of a moment in which placement warrants neither gloam nor ground...

φ

Having never once imagined it, you'll notice that the project of imagining imagining it is sufficiently compelling to follow to its end—to the completion of the project of imagining completion of the project, of the *aim to aim*—a dispatch that would equally put a stop to the imagining of...of that *state of affairs* itself. Have you failed yet? I think not. I think, that is, that you need not concern yourself with such base valuation—or even the discernment of those *modes* of valuation that might serve you once you've steered another course. All endeavors of the kind are just as likely to prove failures...

φ

It's still *my* tale we're on about, whatever your attempts to recreate...to recreate my vain attempts at recreation have portended in their passage towards continual...*eventual* surrender to unwavering requite. As though I've made it clear that such a genesis is happening, or has happened yet...

φ

What can I say. I've tried my hand at conjuring examples, the general exposition of *commonalities*, of inferred designs; I've attempted to come clean in exploration of the fullness of the average man as he lives out his average day, but all I have...all I seem to have *accomplished* is a detailing of absences still inherent at present—still hidden in the image of what's happening...

φ

I have left myself few options, it may be, but that's how the pursuit of such replete verisimilitude happens—one tries one's hand until one gains some measure of attainment, or finds no other method to conceive of such result. It may come in the very intervention of the aim, or it may take some parley on the factors that make *this* image so difficult to limn, but the effort remains equal insofar as its procedure has proceeded towards inertia—towards *preferment* ...

φ

It is *assuredly* the case that if one executes some stratagem ideally but still finds oneself at distance from one's postulated end, one can dismiss that practice from one's subsequent approaches, a narrowing of options that transports one ever closer to some *cardinal* supervenience—one's hope of overcoming every battle with its rout...

φ

My options may be few, but they will still induce me towards the *promise* of solution—as they have, I think I've shown, up to this point. I take my present state of mind as paradigm—so *reference*—in thrall to which that *former* state appears to be complete; as such, I ought have a way to offer up the way that led me from that erstwhile anguish, if it can yet be proffered as a fathomable plight...

φ

A way, I might well add, that seemed to countenance the hodge-podge of this lyric reminiscence to begin with, as it still does today. No longer exclusively so, but that is not my business; or while it's no one *else's* business, it's still not the business—even the *sort* of business—I'm conducting now. My concern with present purposes may reveal...may *have revealed* the many ancillary motives I've acquitted on my path, but I'm still willing to pursue them only insofar as they suggest not merely provenance, but consummation...

φ

When I awoke to find myself...to *be within* that absence, for lack of any clearer—or more *prescient*—turn of phrase, my first thought was to grasp for some...for *any* minor detail that might somehow prove familiar in its function or its dictate, but I simply couldn't find one, or at the least the forms I found could hardly be called functions in the world. It seemed to be a nearly *synaesthetic* disinterment, distinguished from all similar derangements of the scene by neither marking nor avoiding any one sense in particular; by leaving no sense *out* to serve as ground. The confusion of such otherwise discriminate receptors may straightway have required that my sense of their distinction disappear, but it equally suggested their essential contiguity in relation to the inner I remained and remain still...

φ

It's not that I sensed nothing; I looked out and saw the shapes of many...the rise and fall of many disparate shapes before me, the square and then the circle of some...well, at that point of some thing or things I could not yet identify in practice or in turn. That still seemed unintelligible in turn. Incitement into such a state proved central to my consciousness of having lost my way by having lost all sense of such a way plainly discerned, a notion that requires something *like* a world...

φ

How can I put it. Perhaps I ought to give up and move on. And so I speculated then, in that impalpable surrounding, when every intimation of an outside I could muster excited but a *guess* at the construction of the scene to come. I knew that I was somewhere, that *some* world stretched beyond me, but I still had no notion of its character of congress with the world in which I lay...I had laid down...

φ

And then it hit me—such constancy had yet to frame a want or expectation, and so I could not bring to mind a previous or parallel pursuit. Of some still distant past I was aware *in general*, but I could see no intercourse between such bygone *situ* and that amorphous footing that confined me then and there. I awoke within an ocean I alone would chance to swim, my corpse preserved and twitching in a quagmire of forms; I was a sterile bog man held together by the tar, and never to inspirit feckless odes...

φ

Oh, how very droll, a sort of idle reflex. Imagining myself arrayed across *some* trammeled amplitude—some plenary proportion, if not a tempered scale—presented the advantage of persisting as I had been, insofar as having been can be called being once it's so. I was there, as I've averred, and there I knew that I was something, but not by some mere exercise of cogitative skill. I knew that I was body, that my corpulence abounded, just as it had since I awoke, a slash across the vellum of the void...

φ

So the incredulity that marked my dispossession bore no likeness to the peal of doubt made credo by the sage; so the disbelief that first engendered this perdition differentiates the sort of unconcern I was suborned to—forced to suffer when...

φ

In *my* case, I had neither willed such method into consciousness nor mapped its fractured bulwark on the schema of a world, presently palpated or inferred by some palpations still to come; in my case, it came on me, when propelled into a waking dream I found no other other than the other that *received* no other thus to call my own—no world to bracket out by feeble coup of intellection, but only the extension into absence that my complement of viscera unwittingly maintained. I knew that what was there was not the only there there was, but equally that there would be...there *must* be some there there to settle *into*, as it were; that something there would intimate the bourne of an encompassing, a cincture yet to be revealed by some extrinsic goad. I knew that I was there, and with this know-how...

φ

One may act within the rubric of the method so described, allowing only what is deemed indubitable for ground, and employing
that procedure one may indeed conclude that every act of cogitation
holds prerequisite a cogito—a thinker thinking of itself, the self that
it acts *through*. The problem, it appears to me—or seemingly it *has*
now that I've lived its counterpose—is that one never once succeeds
in plucking cogitation from the fitful extensivity it cogitates upon;
that the seity attempting to enact such an abridgment can't exempt
itself from sensing those same forms that it excludes...

φ

What's decidedly uncertain may no less fail to evidence the hook on
which one's epistemic guideline is belayed, and thereby one can use
it to establish the utility of the pose, but there remains a difference
between such ambiguity and the indubitable rejection of the claim
that leads it on...it takes for ground...

φ

To put it simply—not knowing for certain is not knowing for certain
not, and it's this equivocation that constitutes the fallacy such com-
pulsive doubt commends. If, that is, one leaves behind the need for
*exposition*, then one can well be certain that—*congruent* with one's
claims—one has still had the sense of *something*, something whose
restatement as a statement in the first place can't be adduced a certainty, which is to say can't be determined *false* by proof of some contrary strain—the contraindication that it's contrary implies...

φ

One lives within a circumstance by granting certain certainties, certainties that have not yet been verified, it seems; one can't help but
assume some claims are certain that are not so in the course of one's

persistence as an actor in the world. That said, *my* contingency—the portent whose accession first consigned me to this trail—proved utterly decisive to my placement in the landscape that same portent seems to clearly disavow...

φ

What I'm trying to avoid is all temptation to consider the occurrence I'm recounting as an exercise—a *ruse*—and not the very stimulus I was on that occasion first occasioned to consider altogether of extrinsic source. The situation, it appeared, embodied more than the mere absence of familiar or indubitable grounds; indeed, I soon believed that that uncertainty was just as much the character of my delinquent personage as the characterization of the scene thereby corralled. It was *not* some failed attempt to find the terms on which to base some crudely ponderous surmise, but rather signaled my acceptance that one need no such foundation to build onto, that one might just as well befoul the field with salt as seed...

φ

Yes, I was not comfortable...not *comforted* by cognizance of where or even what I was or seemed, but neither was I overwhelmed by any sort of anguish, a state of mind I'd later come to recognize I'd reveled in when no such obfuscation of the forms of things—myself not least among them—was at play. In this regard my *first* return to certainty was the recollection that, all things considered, things could well be worse—that they *had* been, it seemed fair to say, and so they could be still...

φ

Not that I had reason to expect some new disaster to befall me. I merely understood that it was possible—that I could well have found myself abandoned to this bafflement with the consequent adoption of a mood far less desirable than this. Than the pose that I affected at that moment, unflinching though it seemed. And even if it turns out that in retrospect I *couldn't* have, for never having done so...

φ

Never having done so may suggest I couldn't have, but merely *recollecting* having lived through harder times ought give me hope, at least divert me from despondency. Apparently without the verve to bring me back into the world, but that's not everything. Most things, maybe. But not all...

φ

I was not exactly comfortable, but neither did I panic, despite not having had the chance to apprehend the differences between that fateful circumstance and what had come before—a recollection not of any singular occasion, but only the occasion of my sensing such a barrier, the veil between what has been and what's presently in view. I did not want particular remembrances of particular events, just as those that then confronted me required no precise delineation to seem far less compellingly repulsive to my sense of breach or place, and so my slight relief at having managed to avoid the plight could not serve to facilitate my forthcoming escape. As something to hold onto, anything at all that might assemble a presentiment of a world that's *coming on*, regardless of the gaze I hold...that I should be found *holding to* within it...

φ

I'd begun to feel the tender lips of personage nip playfully at heel, I'd seen coteries of shadows merge in geometric fields, but I had only just remembered that such difference from the world would need secure a greater rupture than my merely *feeling* certain of a yet amorphous agency, a *self* to which all other sensitivities defer; that I was still more different from the world in which I wallowed than merely being as myself merely implies...

φ

I am not merely as myself, but presently I'm *in* myself, and think-ing so I realized what the problem...with what discrete *exigency* my problem could be solved. I must not only know that I am something, something *somewhere*, but must divine a way to understand myself—and so my *understandings*—as though other, as though *else*. In order to be in a world held true to what it seems—or what it *did* seem, just as it seems still...

φ

In order to be in a world I must not be equivalent to all its disparate parts; in order to be in a world *with others*—with any other singular contrived as being in—I must be likewise singular, distinct within the total in whose margins I'm displayed...

φ

This may not yet appear an irrefutable conclusion; it's a matter of discernment, of the nature of discernment; it's nothing but a matter of the nature of discernment, conceived of as an act that acts upon what it descries. All such cogitative feint can't help but to distin-guish...but *require* some like object—requires an object, rather, not merely something like one, whether taken as the ego whose aware-ness is in question or a set that includes everything else. Everything but. Everything immured in a perspective...

φ

It is my understanding, or it *was*, I should make clear—it's more im-portant that it was than that it is so now, though it is...I understood that all my many failed attempts to realize such unshakable acuity, discounting how ingenious or obscure they may have seemed, could not be thought consistently and singly directed, or could not *be* so, whether *thought* as such or no. I do not merely act upon the world that I survey through the activity of surveillance—thus discerning it as something that's discernible, that is—but am also acted *on* by that same substance I allege as both its order and its terminus; I am as much receiver of the world as its determinant, a manifold to which I stand as other else again...

φ

As adjunct to the set for which I no less act as bracket, I must take in some...some substance—some *constituents*—from which to make the making of the world that I receive, that *receives me*; a world at once inclusive of the activity of receipt...

φ

What I want to say is...ah, what a bother. I grow weary of...of myself. And yet I have no remedy but...

φ

What I'm trying to assert is that the incidental limits of the organs of sensation must intractably distinguish me from all that I receive, that if I want to turn my gaze out towards the hazy substance whose equivalence I seem to have remained through all my supplemental yearnings and impulsions—still making the distinction between selfdom and its outside...and any outside manifestly lodged within the scene—then I can only...only...

φ

I need to find the bound, I thought, that makes discernment possible, that manifests as precursor to understanding anything as one or thing at all; I need discern the *border* between what's in and its outer, the line I draw between myself and all that I receive. And where might one begin to look for such a vagile margin? Where is it most evident that *I* am now a thing in turn distinguished from its otherwise, from everything I can't help but think otherwise...

φ

That everything is surface is a truth I'd long accepted—it did not make me *feel* that I had somehow lost my way—but that I could sense anything, in any frame or circumstance, that I could only claim a surface insofar as its continuum betokened my distinction from the field in which I lay...Such was the peculiar correspondence that compelled me from that waking dream...

φ

It was all becoming clear; my path to *clarity*, that is to say, was clearing up before me, arising as a vision of...of...And so again I found my egress blocked at every turn. It was a vision of envisioning, of how I'd *feel* should I release myself from that...that *discipline*, I'll concede, but even *trying* to describe it as a state of mind or circumstance required its distinction from some equal claim, some claim to come...

φ

To span the wayward span whose border stands to stand beside it; to imagine some endeavor to imagine, to *conceive*, an image still no closer to what makes up—so what augurs—that imagining itself...

φ

I must be in possession of determinable margins—at least *some* wayward carcass must surround me, I believed—and that pulsating figure had begun to feel its station, to yield to the impression of accountable demesne. I had a sense of form, of some determinable *out*side, a shape I couldn't even say I'd failed to find an image of, for never having had the aim to image it before...

φ

Yes, I was all surface at that point—*within that torment*—despite my inability to trace its slumping line, and having thus regained...*re-membered* to look for myself...look *at* myself looking for myself just there, resigned to languish, I began at once to feel it, to have a sense of bound...of binding *substance* held contiguous with its outside, a throbbing gust across the broad expanse of marching cilia that swaddled the integument I'd suddenly attained. I sensed that there was something slowly happening about me, the suppliant resistances of scales and scrapes and scabs...

φ

I itch, I thought, all over, but at points upon my surface—it *seemed* I could discern each discrete apogee in turn. I was instantly aware that I had more than one sensation, even as I recognized no more than one at once. If only I could...But I'm not there yet. Or I wasn't. I wasn't at that moment, and so I'm not within this surging chronicle of my plight—the plight to which that posture stands as prefatory index, the dreamed conceit of sublimating cause...

φ

Itching suggests dermis to upbraid, that's what I theorized, and though I couldn't stop myself from such vague stipulation I knew that doing so need not result in something more—something like transitioning to animus, to action; something that might soon assuage that suppurating scourge. I knew that thinking *of* it wasn't quite the same as *doing* it—that thinking of doing and doing are different doings, different *modes*—and while this may appear to you not much of a conclusion...not much *insight*, I should say, as I had yet no reason to conclude I was concluding...

φ

I did not draw conclusions based on premises accepted; I was not yet aware of any actionable aim. At one moment I had no sense that I was in position...in position in a place that one could hold position *in*, and next I knew that something...I *sensed* the seeming surface of my bulk in an environ, but what that was, or where it was, or how it could explain...I sensed that I was there—or so I'd tacitly exacted— for having the extent of my extension there displayed; I knew that with extension comes the space that one extends through, that one can't press out into...can't fill anything but...

φ

But that's beside the point, you say, and I couldn't agree more. You understand, I see, that if there is indeed a point then there must be a point beside it; you've understood the point without my lead— without my *prodding;* before you came upon my pointing *to* it, and so you can't resist the thought that I have nothing to reveal. You may be right. You may, that is, have nothing much to learn from my so- licitous conclusions, but my *methods* of concluding them are surely not so frequently encountered on your way, and it remains my hope that this proves proof enough of benefit to continue to afford me your commitment...your *attention*, which is to say your ongoing concern...

φ

You balk that it may not be, and I'm happy to report I don't be- grudge you the complaint—not because I'm in agreement, but be- cause your thinking so is of no consequence, no matter that you're proven right or wrong in future course. What danger in surrender- ing the benefit of the doubt, whether offered here to me or left to drift to someone else? There is no point not rightly thought to rest beside another...

φ

That I found an itch to scratch—to think as *scratchable*, perhaps—already seemed a triumph, or it *would* have done if it had stopped right there. Triumph enough to...to do what, I'm not certain; it seemed a stable foothold at the base of an escarpment, where formerly I'd had no sense of obstacle or bar...

φ

Discernment of a place upon my husk—my *superficies*—gave me hope that I might know what that field stands *against*. It is the nature of the surface, that it should designate an alter, establishing a space filled up with similarly outlived forms. Yes, I told myself, I've yet to palpate that estate to which I'm seemingly appended, but I can still declare that I've discerned it's churning glut; that I am shut within it, so that it remains *in reach*...

φ

And what *am* I, I wondered, the interior or the surface? Is the surface what prevents me from all commerce with an inner that is not at once inside—that holds me at the surface of *this* inside, as it were? Where am I in reference to the borders thus imparted? That seem to give my purview its insuperable range? I can't say. Or I couldn't. What I can or can't say now is not at issue. What I'm *saying* now may yet be, but what else I *could* have said...

φ

I felt a nascent sense of...of the *sensitivity* of my surface, and so I understood that only chance excoriation could portend some more than *possible* relief. I could do well, I thought, to make use of some portion of that surface that plays victim to such aggregative stimulus to excoriate *itself*, an involution, it seemed sure, that was...that is...that is and was a commonplace, if not exactly commonplace to me just at that point. The problem still had nothing much to do with my conception...my *ability* to conceive of my corporeal subsistence over distant ground and near, but rather that in thinking so I could not find—*had not yet found*—the palimpsest on which to trace that limen in its margins, its thus far unimaginable field...

φ

I had an itch, and then another. I had many all at once, but my perception of each one was nonetheless completely singular, as though a map upon which only one point could be marked...

φ

There may be one such irksome node, I thought, there may be many. It's clear, I told myself, that one's impressions often lie. And yet I could not understand the itch that's perceived wrongly—that proves *illusory*; that at long last reveals itself as not an itch at all, but still another stimulus, if not another kind. Still another kind of stimulus...

φ

I can imagine the discovery of phenomena coincident with that initial goad, giving weight to the assertion that the itch is an *effect*, but unlike other rather common misimpressions—the line bent by some artful lens, the echo that appears another voice—it was still precisely there, just where it was when it was extant...when I *thought* that it was extant, and it was precisely gone when I could feel it there no more...

φ

Of course one can conceive of other inference from the fact of some sense *felt*, inference that proves mistaken when put to the test; I can readily appropriate some adventitious stimulus into an etiology to which it proves extrinsic upon second or third glance, but the fact that I feel something—and not *merely* something, but *this* thing in particular—is not subject to debate. Even the *location* of the sense can't be refuted if that refutation vows it was erroneously sensed, and not just thought to be somewhere that it turns out it's not; that its vigor should diverge with shift in perch or punctuation...

φ

And can one generalize this claim to other feeling states? Can the dreamer be thought false to his intrinsic affectations—to what he always presently *perceives* as his response? Is it possible to dream one has a pain while at one's ease, without an ache? Or an itch when no such spur offends the corpus of the dreamer—alone made sense, that is to say, while moldering in sleep? One thus mistakes narration of events as they're occurring with the occurrence of the events themselves—the occurrence of narration with the bearing of the world that is made narrative therein. Or thereby...

φ

If one is fearful in one's dreams then that fear is not semblance; the cause may be some stimulus within the dream alone, but the sentiment aroused is just as real as any that's occasioned by events set in the world outside. In dreams, what feels like itching—or any other stimulus one can construe as sensed—is always as the *present* excitation of one's somnolent avatar, if not the state in which one's figure wallows dull and dazed...

φ

Absent any other certainty, one can be sure of this; what's set within the rubric of some given field of sense is always rightly thought a stimulus—is not, as such, *delusion*—as only it's position in the scene can be mistook. One may well feel a twinge upon a limb that's long since lost, and though it seems self-evident that the inference is false the impression of an itch just there, in space once occupied...space that *would* be occupied by some untoward appendage were it presently appended to the one who feels its ghost is a veracity that needs no further proof. *Prurito ergo sum...*

62

φ

Having chanced upon what seemed the very *certainty* of extension, I could concentrate more fully on the task at hand. No. That's not it. Having *given myself over* to the fact of my extension, I was able to examine...to begin to draw the bounds...I began what seemed to me would be the process of transfiguring my sense of being in place in accordance with my placement, following my outline to the world whose difference *from* it such assemblage invariably endues...

φ

It's peculiar to think this way, I know. Peculiar, that is, to understand the brackets of a set as the determinant for all that lies beyond it—to use what's *in* to map a world *essentially* outside. Which is not to say the peculiarity of a notion, whatever it may be, ought steer anyone from anything; at worst such crude anomaly makes it more difficult to take me at my word. To take aim at my word, when my word seems so aimless...

φ

The peculiarities of my character must appear to you self-evident, so the consequent peculiarities of my insight—of my *attempts* at insight—should come as no surprise. I am myself no longer apprehensive for that deviance, but I don't tell you this for fear you'll soon be tempted to some hostile counterclaim; I do so as a way of making *my* sense of said strangeness seem familiar—*not strange*; to make my sense of strangeness seem familiar...

φ

Still I must conciliate this posture of conformity with the sense of the exception that I've only just recalled—that such a strangeness bears no one relation to the clarity by which it idly happens to surrender its remove, although for you this nuance may well drift beyond

63

the pale. Precisely why this is...

φ

But no—I will not do this now. I will not do this now. Let them come. Come to you, I say. Me, I mean. By you I mean me. Or I. You mean I and I mean me, so when I voice the speaker who is speaking from the outside, I do not mean myself, but that I that has come to seem another you—as me or I—*to* you, to you I say...

φ

My insights may prove too abstruse to pause before repeating them—before even *including* them within that parted viscera whose frame I hope to fill...to *proffer* as the self for whom I've born the selfless burden of these vagrant bounds...

φ

And though I have experienced that feeling of the alien—so the fetter of pursuing my queer megrims to their ends—I've grown accustomed...I've accustomed *myself* to this sense of my strangeness and suggest you do the same if you intend to soldier on. Or you *will have done so* should you somehow manage to abide me, whether such endurance proves to be a conscious act or no. It seems a petty lark that such a strangeness should come on us...should *distract* us from the object that first sanctioned the refrain, when that object is the strangeness of...of anything, really; any world that one could call distinct from that...from that in which I...any world distinguished from the sump in which *I* live...

φ

The world in which I live is not made other to its obverse—to its transverse or its obverse—merely for its merely being thought so, so I thought, although such thinking *of* it may prove inconsistent with the thinking that's within it, just the same. I tried to implicate the age in which I had projected...*through* which I had *deduced* my yet orthogonal pruritus as though what would restore me to my rightful place within it was its only unique charm—its singular distinction as that world that I've singularly managed to address, thus an allocution forming more than some mere part of its design. Such claim at once presenting the circularity of the pose—the circularity *of the circumference*...

φ

All that differentiates this world from all the others—the others that it could have been, perhaps could still—is that it's made realizable...made *possible* by having thus been realized; distinguished by its having been distinguished, having *been discerned*. Somehow, the apparent singularity of my form had in common with all other sums I'd come to hold as *true* the readily conceded fact of my inclusion in it, even as its character remained unknown...

φ

Why would one require the completion...the complete *iteration* of the members of a set in order to distinguish any one such idle term—to count oneself within it or beyond its fettered ken? The set of primes is not inscribed by one prime in particular, but includes every last cipher of that infinite it culls. So am I *within* the world, although I can't declaim its contents; a world whose members I'm among but whose *membership* remains *inexorably* obscure...

φ

Still, I told myself, there must be *some* way to continue—it's what such inner monologue obliges, as a creed; to continue on the path towards the complete enumeration of what's nonetheless essentially innumerable...

φ

The set I longed to catalogue was *itself* made singular...was constituted as a set—as curried into bounds—by my existence in it as depo-
nent, as *surveyor*; as agent of it's ever indeterminate account. I can't
say such conclusion proved particularly happy, or that it yet appeared
a turn upon the course that it vaguely presumed, but still I understood that I had given myself over to a membership which promised
at the least the possibility of others in its aspect—in the midst of its
assembly, its *surmise*...

φ

This return to multiplicity seemed where I always had been, as
though I hadn't retrogressed for never having left. All I need do now,
I thought, is gather up the vestiges...the *residue* of what had most assuredly preceded as a residue of what had most assuredly preceded...

φ

Let us think it this way, by way of thinking that our way of thinking
makes a sum; the world I'm in is first and foremost stipulated equal
to the world that's left once I'm subtracted from it—once I've first
accounted for the set of my own predicates, a set I've always already
extended to its final term—revealing that the object of that bracket-
ing mathesis should abide only as possible, as a concept of the possible...

φ

The actual is assuredly a subset of the possible—a member of the *set*
of all that's possible, that is—but that I am *myself* another adjunct of
that aggregate does little to give voice or shape to anything but...but
what is giving voice by giving voice *to* at this instant, the voice whose
echo intimates this instant now it's lost...

φ

If only such reflection could reveal what's missing from it—the *what* I'd have to indicate before I could move on...It's all we ever want, each fit and tied to her own station, to continue the continuance of what has never once met the conditions *any* claim to continuity requires, which are...

φ

Stop yourself right there, I thought, or so I think I might have had this sort of inner pageant been my practice at the time. I can't say for a certainty it wasn't, although it seems rather improbable...It must surely seem improbable—or so it seems to me—that I could have compiled such a list of provocations when I first came to be so indissolubly provoked—the moment that that happening was *happening within*. Not moment—*situation*; in the course of recognizing what my situation was, which in this case would amount to—*did* amount to, I should say—the release from those conditions that contrived it, which were...

φ

Again, it seems unlikely all I've garnered in the service of...of this jejune description of my actual...my *manifest* escape from that odd plight is all *in fact* I used in making that transcendence of transcendence—that transcendence *into immanence*—a wherewithal, thus real. It may be that my innovation then was not without resemblance to what I'm here inclined to think my innovation then; that what I'm here inclined to think my innovation then is not entirely unlike what that then innovation was...

φ

It's clear to me that what I'm thinking now that I thought then is more properly akin to what I'm thinking now, now that I think of my thoughts then in present term. I know there was a reason...that *I had my reasons* for evoking such a distant and inadequately understood surmise—inadequate for it's character as nothing more than that, than an endless cogitation on that provocation then, and so its superlatives, which are...which have been...

φ

Ah, yes, that's what it was. I was attempting to *relate* my yet ambiguous remembrance of the moment I began to know my talents, so my ends; the first I came to realize that the spray of silent sunlight could arrest the dissolution of the world in which...*to* which I had awoken and so bring about a claim to purpose presently—to purposes *revealed* while in the midst of their pursuit. I returned...I was *attempting* to return my thinking now to what I deigned think now back then, back when I decided to return to the inception of the organon that's come to represent me as I am, as I have been...

φ

It is an odd characteristic of such present sensibilities—such purposes *presented* as a portent of the now—that any first attempt at explanation *or* description first requires a remembrance and description of the first it can be presently...that it can be *recalled*, in turn, as having been at present; the first, that is, that it was in a present time revealed...

φ

And equally significant to such perverse design, the picture of the *coming on* of any scene must indicate...must seemingly *presume* its ancillary predicates—what borders that continuum and where those borders lie. It is a fact that if one wants to claim some circumstantial sheen as singular—as extant and extended through the given scene at all—one must account for its bygone transition from some other...some other *anything*, absent which one can't conceive of either form *or* absence, whether such conception serves us now as précis, or as tale...

φ

And why should this be understood as uniformly so? What gives the prime this cast in the translation...the *redaction* of our everlasting toil, either present to its maker or beyond the present pale? It's a question of logic, not ontology—the problem of advancing such an analogue of primacy once we've seen its repetition once or countless times before. But I could be wrong. I'm not sure what distinguishes existence *as* event from merely being in the form that such event takes for its...its...

φ

Let me start again. No, don't fret, not *everything*, just what every precedent requires to put...to *have* put this *present* present in its present form. Let us try a sort of...a manner of *experiment* is what I have in mind, though you will play no greater role than witness to the gest. What more could you expect. Or what else. If you're thinking clearly, you know you have no other choice, even as I play your part in this peculiar courtesy—the feigned dissimulation of the same delayed...

φ

What would you have me do. What can either of us...*any* of us do to counteract the act of voice...of voicing...the act of making voice out of some voicing that our posture commends. Nothing, I say. There may have been options, but not for me. All *I* have is this conceit of address—of *undirected* address—for the promise of a promising...of a *probable* surrender to requite. Or if it *is* directed, it's only *from* and never towards; a focal barb that drifts in an immeasurable...

φ

I would like to take this moment to digress from my digressions in the name of every addressee still reachable by writ, every interlocutor screwed up to the decipherment of this inane amusement—what amounts to little more than random scratches in the dirt. I may as well admit that I'm among just such a cohort, and in the act of leading hope to stumble back to cause. To *my* cause; the cause that I've so easily...so *seamlessly* abandoned, even as abandonment appeared its proper... its *only* course...

φ

Imagine that your interests, insofar as you're still with me, are for all intents and purposes identical to mine, that any further variance is of no real importance to our future sense of partnership, however you may yet conceive your agency disjoined...

φ

Imagine that some change of state is happening this instant, that you are reaching out into fruition, as it were, where every last...every *previous* attempt had seemed but one step closer to some ripening on the vine. There is a signal moment—or there *must* be, it appears—when you can claim with certainty that such act is completed, and should you find yourself disposed to chronicle the passage you would first need mark its difference from your now *erstwhile* position as though it were a breakthrough that the foregoing entails...

φ

But can this be the *only* way to stake one's claims to claim? It's possible to postulate the newness of a new life in its new world without reference to a previous, a former state whose inner works might never have achieved such term but for the illustration of new bounds...

φ

It's just this mode of discourse—of *delinquency*—I'm after; to tell you...to even *try* to tell you what my life was like...what *life*, that is, was like before I had awaked—well, the pose seems near as difficult as pointless, both for knowing just how little I have left of that old life and how irrelevant that life is to me now. What matters is not how I could have lived a life that, in retrospect, seems wholly indistinguishable from...seems wholly *undistinguished*, but what—given its genus—differentiates it's aftermath, the life I've come to think of as the one I *ought* to live...

φ

This may seem contradictory—in fact it may well be—to those who can't discriminate the limit from its precincts, from what the sense of boundary *binds in* to such surveil. Discovering the threshold of one's reach, it stands to reason, does little to characterize the unreachable, even as it demonstrates the existence of the same. Someday one might undertake to chart its nether regions, should one ever have the privilege to traverse its dips and swells, or it might seem so alien to one's provincial idiom that it eludes all practicable sense of reason or accord, but for all that the *scale* of the beyond makes little difference...

φ

Thus I have contrived to mark the moment that my life changed—at which I became *myself*, a match of aim to view. Such peculiar circumstance is made so—both peculiar *and* circumstance—by the act of overcoming it in some way that portends...that in this instance *portended* what was soon to come to be me, to be the me that I've been since, the me who's speaking now...

φ

That I was there—*that there was I*—before reaching that pass may seem the sort of certitude one can't refuse to grant, but just like every other fool who claims some tacit origin in an infancy occluded by subsequent events, I was unaware of its conditions and unable to conceive of any path to their discovery at some future point. That moment of transgression *was* my natal bearing, it's all that I can muster as an augur of said pulse, and for each such coalescence into personhood I come upon it serves me as both archetype and measure, a standard that's proved mastery time and again...

φ

There I lay, a flaccid cramp, no hold to gain resistance—to make the world a rupture from all inkling of its range. I'd managed, as I've shown, to resurrect the claim to being *in* without which no alterity can surface as a framework, but only as I found my senses bounded by an exigence interior to my amplitude—to every muffled flutter of my torso, or my limbs...

φ

There was, it soon emerged, a sort of *out* in which I foundered—*into* which my saltatory aggregate arrayed—but while that proved a first step on the way back to the open...the opening of seity to what it stands *against*, that pose remained all surface, nothing but the claim to surface...I had only found a surface to suggest what might be other than...be other...to indicate an other that could equally be in...

φ

And while it may be tempting to believe my weakened powers of analysis were at fault, such belief would be mistaken. Not that I think they—my powers, that is—wouldn't be inadequate to pursuing other ends, but it's my claim that no similarly constituted faculties would be better suited to *this* project, which is to say could make the slightest difference in the character *or* ascendancy of my many failed attempts at such account. Not claim; I want to say conclusion—or so I'm saying, here and now, debarring I want. That I'm saying what I'm

72

saying may suggest I'd *rather* say it, but I've been guilty of such truck when in truth I'd rather not. That you have been made subject...been *subjected to* deception...

φ

It's obvious to me the trouble isn't my description so much as it's inherent in the plenum I describe, a state that may prove unfamiliar to your station, without any clear referent to the present...to any state that's present, or set within the present mind...

φ

How can one begin to speak of what one can't refer to? What only serves as referent if it's referent is a *lack*? One may allude to deficits—to moments passed and chances lost—but how speak of an absence of *everything*, of every *possible* mark? How recall a nature whose one singular refinement is found in apposition to a void of every nature, the transient propinquity of an itch that can't be scratched? How can one begin...

φ

It's difficult to describe because it had no outside; because, without an outside, there are no events...no *constants*, and without some sort of constant there's no way to mark a bound. Does this assertion stand as any less than universal? At least so far as it applies to every property of...of things that can have properties; in the realization that an absence of properties, in the absence of a contrary, is nothing more or less than the absence of all reference *to* properties, in this case made available by the action of remembering its predicates before said absence could arise. All to say that if you think my explanation... my *attempts* at either explanation *or* description disconcerting, then you can well imagine the extent to which I found myself similarly abashed—a reason, I would hope, to soon conciliate the spite...

φ

It is interesting *to note* that this...this...I was going to say story...fable...*course of events*, but no such phrase captures the ambivalence of my project, whatever that may seem or seem to point to as a future path. Interesting, that is, that in the project of projecting myself back upon the circumstance from which I once thrust forward into this life I lead now I've stumbled on a mode of expectation for which both explanatory and descriptive undertakings are not only equally difficult—even worthless—but actually identical, whether seen in whole or part...

φ

It is the very pretense of originary modes—of the primal singularity, the first before the first—that leaves one without difference...without foil or divide, so requiring appraisal of the *absence* of such difference as the first line of description, also the last...

φ

What's *provocative*, that is to say, is that this understanding—this broad *equivocation*, as I think I've long since proved—is my first attempt at referencing the absence *in its own terms*—without merely referring to the absence *of awareness* that suggested the recitative from which this dream arose. No matter how inadequate my characterization of the absence of character may appear, you would be mistaken if you thought I could do better...could do *else*...

φ

What other artifact of consciousness can be construed ostensive by such parsing of an affect, such birthing of a way? My hand has certain digits, each articulated at the crease of muscled joints; it rests upon a pedestal festooned with blocks of inky black, in regular and signatory contrast to the whitewashed wood which burnishes the surface

74

of its pickled bulk. My flabby hand is pressing flabby fingertips to palm, attempting to relieve the cramp this scrawl has brought about. So where, in this portrayal, are the predicates that designate my circumstance *presented*? And accepting such an abstract of said traits in their array, is the sense of that array *itself* described in more than instrumental part? In part more than instrumental...

φ

I think you see my point—judge for yourself. The point that this attempt at such a portrait of the absence...of the *rising out of absence* with which my life burst seemingly to presence and to form has since demanded of its limner the insuperable mingling of explanation and account, that each in turn must be attended by an intimation of the other, whether understood as happening or...

φ

I think, seeing my point, as now I'm *sure* you do...you must...whether or not you must, you do, or the other way around...I think, that is, you still can't find the point my point *points out*. Where, for instance, has either explanation or account entered into my dissembled recall of awaking in that whilom vale—that foregone plaint? Be patient. Or don't. You may find that you're satisfied anon. Or not...

φ

Where was I. That's what I'm trying to say. To *prove* that I was somewhere when I left off saying where I was to say that where I was was not yet known. I've decisively established—or I *had*, stuck in that pose—that I was just then extant as addendum to the itch that crawled across my ported bodice, tracing thus its boundaries, its impermeable germ. It's not that all at once I was aware of that gelled skinscape, but rather was discretely made aware of my awareness, outside of all acuity in fathoming the scene. As though I had construed some sort of figure I could trace against...against...against

75

*anything.* I hadn't, let me be perfectly clear, but if I had such measure would be no concern of mine. Or it wouldn't have been, where it might well be now if it were so when it began...

φ

There must, I thought, be up, there must be down, there must be one side and its obverse; if I extend...if I merely *feel* that I'm extended there must be something to extend towards; if I'm able to reach out there must be something to reach into, even though it should remain abidingly obscure. Such base realization that there *was* a certain portion of my person that extended—or that there might have once been, in some previous milieu—requires that there be a space conceived of in its absence, a space I would have occupied had I been in the present so disposed...

φ

I wallowed in the margins of some integrated amplitude, and any such assemblage must be somewhere, at some point plotted on the map of places not just possible, but real. How, then, to move forward with the goal of its discernment? How make of my prurience a way back to the world? But this was not my question, or not strictly how I put it; not how I *recall* it being put...

φ

I did not really ask myself to palpate my location, to yet consider moving arm or fingertip or thigh, when presently I found the silence breaking—I felt the opening of the open, and the scattering of the gone. I can't say how it came to me, or how I came upon it; something just came over me, or off...something that preceded my return to holding place within that involuted affect, requiring the resumption of a privilege...of a *course* I had no reason to suspect was mine to hold, at least in that small portion of a life I could allow that I'd experienced before...before that moment. I surely need not say that what comes after...what comes after is continued...

φ

And what exactly was it, you ask? What induced me *out of* and so *into* this odd stupor of kinetic modes, modes *over*determined when considered from the standpoint of one's singular commencement, of one's only standing start? It was the pull of that peculiar...that *once* peculiar, now quite common luminescence, the swaddle of reflections that enraptured my recline. There it was, a blinding flash, but equally a pinpoint, a squint into the shadows and a flit across the retina notwithstanding...

φ

I seem to be incapable of capturing the moment—of vouchsafing that image of...of how I was incipiently *met*...An odd way to put it, as if that's worth remarking—as if that marks a *difference* from your slog through all the rest. That one can do *anything* in a manner one can fairly call incipient...

φ

I don't know. It seemed right at the time. Good enough, I say, and yet I realize—such explanation isn't even good enough for me. I was beginning something, something that I claim to have continued since. The world, it now appears, had opened up to me in ways both unexpected *and* familiar—unexpected in the wake of its occlusion moments previous, familiar in relation to all former...all former and now abrogated absences of absence, as this time was the first and last I'd find myself so brazenly dispensed. It's not that there was light where there had formerly been darkness—or while this was a feature of that circumstantial break, the activity of receiving such effulgence doesn't capture...doesn't *justify* my singular response to the event. As though such an event and the response that it engenders are at odds...can be *distinguished*...

φ

The world was thus illumined, was undeniably *turned on* where it had been...where formerly there seemed no ready passage to ascend into discernment. Ascend *from* darkness; that some mere coruscation should take the place of clarity, and clarity stand in for having risen to the truth...

φ

I had an itch I longed to scratch with stiffened thumb or digit, any share of inner out whose leverage I could ply. It's clear to me that in such plainly proximate immersions the locality defined as such—by that it is *immersed*—is only posed distinct by the imperator who reads it...who *feels* it as particular to that setting alone. Any sensitivity not given to the ego as a proper indication of its proper mode is seen by that who undertakes the seeing of it as a fraction of its inner cast surrendered to the district of some irritated bourne, a stimulus whose consequent avowal as extrinsic is only known in contrast to the unity it marks as the dispute, as the *remainder*...

φ

It is only by convention—by a trick of common parlance—that one understands some symptomatic overlay as part...as intimation of the *whole* to which it stands as part. Consider, for example, a pain at once coincident with some quiescent state and ask yourself how you distinguish such affliction from the agony of heartache, the visceral intensity of *comprehensive* loss. I'd like to think you'll take this odd command as a performative, requiring no further ploy to make good on the gest, though what will happen if you don't...

φ

The extent to which one understands some twinge as interruptive—as *distraction* from one's practical awareness of all else—is what specifies the difference of that state from any other, such that one is said to be...that one describes oneself as *being in* some pain or not. Equally imagine a sensation that's remitting—that has neither implication for some change in scope or scale nor anticipates a soon to seem recuperative mode—and one's notion of such affect as a predicate of ego or as mere indication of some irritated part is determined by that same *im*partial measure of extent...

φ

Should I convulse in agony or strain in the deterrence of such compelled response, all that draws the notice of the credulous observer is the tangible appearance of an otherwise occluded state; if asked on such occasion if I were *alright* I could well indicate I weren't, even if I knew I would be but a moment hence. I might, that is, feel justified in yielding to distraction, if that distraction faithfully betokens an impression of my practical extent...

φ

And that pain that I'm conscious of that is not so perturbing—that wants for no rejoinder, in action or in thought—I might as well keep to myself, unless such an expression could effect its deliquescence, what one would surely sanction as a laudable result. So, too, the itch; should it append itself to every other feeling state—to every sense I understand as concomitant with it—then one can well proclaim it of considerable extent. But if one merely needs to scratch...

φ

Should I merely need to scratch it but soon realize that such act requires some considerable deformity of reach, then it might seem sufficiently divergent from the common course to generate concern in one's admirers—concern that could occasion some entreaty or rebuke. One could, in time, be asked for an appraisal of one's mettle, and even though by that point the distress may have subsided the character of the query is conditioned by the term of interruption that the treatment of said symptom represents...

φ

What's of most importance to expression of a feeling state is how it will prove bar to any parallel attempt—all other forms of acumen concurrent with the sense—although to claim such value as the purview of expressing only bane is surely false. The sense of joy or pleasure—of ecstatic *jouissance*—is equally impactful to one's typifying countenance, to throwing oneself—or *being thrown*—into the whelming crowd, the *line of sight*...

φ

Any pain I feel is ineluctably exact, whatever the character of its expression, or its absence of expression—the *sublimation* of my desire to express it in some way that's discernible to someone else—but all I ever gather of the suffering of another is the perch of simulacra thrust into the moiling procession of events. It *signifies* an inner state thought of a kind with similarly visceral affections by mere likeness in the practice of pointing, the same I've used to indicate some feeling in myself...

φ

Thus if I would deign disclose a pang within some heated puckering or collop I might think to point to it, or mark off its position on something like a map. I may well choose to point to any anything I'd like—an elbow or a stylus or a horse's ass—and in each case *you* can see just what I'm pointing to, just what I'm pointing *at*; you understand it as I do—can *feel* it as I do—which is to say to both of us it is an *external* account. I am always as the back side of a page assumed continuous with its front; a page that's only ever showing front side, but for that who writes...

φ

What I *can* suggest is the scale of disability some affective state asks *of* me when I'm convened within it, and so do I assume that every similar expression of that consonant arousal corresponds to near equivalent effects in someone else. But is not such expression still a manner of comportment, no more a correlate of the thing that it expresses than the name by which we've chosen to provision its expressive drift? Is the act of keeling over in response to some odd plaint any nearer to the *substance* of that suffering than this or that fraught murmur, notwithstanding any subtlety of gesture or descant? In this, I think you'll find, lies both the crux *and* the escape...

φ

For when I feel an ache as if a knife thrust into flesh and so articulate that sudden jolt by taking short and shallow breaths I am not *trying* to say anything to anyone, for *any* purpose or intent; I am not attempting *anything*—not seeking any further end, nor any clear advance—but merely seem to yield to the response. *Yield*, I say, in order to account for those occasions when I *can* resist—when I *try* to and can claim myself successful in the gest. But when, to the contrary, some unexpected torment throws me from my righteous perch I seem to be unable to distinguish my reaction from the stimulus it claims to represent—what it represents *to me* when I'm the one who's forced to suffer it...

φ

The *performance* of the pain may appear compulsory; may *look to be*, that is to say, an attribute of the sense. But might some other raconteur react in different manner, if not with an entirely discordant cast? Be able to withstand some more or less than I can in the process of acceding to involuntary wont? I have no doubt. What matters is the extent of such resistance—the ability to arrest some near intractable prostration, or the willingness to abandon oneself to it when the sequence is desirable in the least...

φ

This, indeed, is all I'm *ever* interested in knowing, when I'm the one with whom...*to* whom you find yourself determined to confess. You should be so lucky. Or I should. And despite this realization, I'm assured of having never...of never having had the chance...

φ

It occurs to me that you might think I think myself...that I'm trying *to portray* myself as helpless to dissimulate an apathetic affect—to adopt an equilibrium I don't actually possess. Let me set the record straight—I can do just as you can, though who can do it better, and who measure the result...

φ

Such a cozenage of otherwise irresolute veneers constitutes a satisfying leap, and seems within the capability of anyone who makes the claim to judge the claim as true or false, but this, too, serves as further evidence of the point. Should I, come what may, appear to flounder in an agony I can't manage to staunch, you may believe the state *itself* equivalent to that expression, a substitution for the catalyst that renders it as such a patent stress. The pain offers a symptom—not of an invasive strike, but rather of some visceral...some enduringly *hermetic* force. But if on second glance I seem in charge of all my faculties—a seeming you've discerned through an ulterior...an as yet *indeterminate*—if not *quite* ulterior—approach...

φ

Perchance you've caught a glimpse of my complacent visage turned into the earth, a glimpse of features you think *ought* to be contorted but are not; perchance when you return sooner than expected from your urgent search for help I have abandoned all my ardor—am *in command* of all my faculties—an air which one who'd just been in the throes of such an agony could not so soon advance. You think you have a sense of the intrinsic state some outward indication manifests; that you've found objective standard, despite having no access to the character of that inner life in anyone—*for the sake of anyone*—but yourself...

φ

The substance of the matter, as it in turn turns out, turns on the acceptance such a standard as a matter of course. We do not care to live the adventitious pains of others—to have some *perfect* empathy invade our common space of common flesh—rather our indemnity to such generalization—the demonstration of it, in surrender or attack—is entirely instrumental at source...

φ

The suffering of another, I'm struggling to suggest, is indistinguishable from the character of its expression—its *performative* effects—and my pain *in particular* enters into discourse on that very same continuum of impulse and restraint. Here, if nowhere else, we can describe ourselves as creatures *of extent*, disregarding the persuasive claims to inner...to *wholly* inner life our doubt seems to adduce. Or some doubt, really, not the *same* as ours, but not irrelevant to ours, nevertheless...

φ

And do we not seem *somewhat* nearer to progressing? To some measured gain of ground, some apt release? Like we're laying the foundation for some forthcoming catharsis, if not our next pretension to such enfeebled bliss? You'll have to pardon the question...the *interruption* that the question seems to warrant as a choice; take it as an order, if you like. I know that if you are to keep on keeping up you will need benchmarks, and if you take exception for more than the mere instant it would take to take it back—to turn back to my tentative amendments and procrustean revolts—then it's likely your desire to avoid reiteration of these many and lugubriously executed steps in favor of a quick march to the finish, to what you're sure to reckon as the very last...

φ

It's clearly my belief that such defection would be...would *amount* to a mistake, and as it is my tale to tell...as it *appears* my tale to tell and mine alone, my declaration of a common cause has all the postured import of a proven truth. If nothing else you can be sure that I've continued to take the necessary pleasure in your company to explain...to *occasionally* explain the reasons for my having reached some one point or the next. What more do you want...

φ

Or *could* you, even. What more could you ask of such a harried interloper than that she should continue at her own pace, in spite of how confusing her offenses...her *illusory* offenses and retreats have proved as yet. The more that you *might* want, I'd like you to accept, is what I'm giving you by giving you anything, by pretending that your patience in awaiting the receipt of my pronouncements is important to me—is a reason for *pronouncing* them, if not quite sufficient proof...

φ

Such admission, needless to say, is *primarily* unfair to myself; it should be obvious by now that my claimed interest in your interest is more than pretense—than a mere capitulation to some surreptitious want. Why else would I bother—would I not now waste my time with something else? Ah, you think you've got me—or I would if I were in your place; you think that I *have* nothing else, that this reprise alone stems the alluvium of boredom by giving the appearance of wonder, of beginning my adventures with—and *through*—the feint of wonder...

φ

And perhaps, at least in this respect, you're right. Perhaps I've reached a point in life—a life, I might well add, whose pitch and flutter you have no way to assess—where I have nothing else to fill the gaps. Or nothing better. If I have something else to do, it's nothing I've thought better of than this. If it were, then I would do it—the imperative is clear enough. There's always something else that one *could* do....

φ

If I do this here, this now, because *not* doing so would leave me bored and restless—without a sense of purpose to direct my next assault—then presumably I've found a way more interesting than what not doing so would do were I to choose it. And what—what brush against the bar—could warrant such a choice? Herein lies the answer *and* the gist. If, as it turns out, I approach *this* act with interest, even if such interest is not part of what I find it so interesting to confess, then one can reasonably conclude that I am *equally* concerned with its eventual...*continual*, it may well be, but no less *forthcoming* dispatch....

φ

An engagement, you may realize, that amounts to little more than the tautology of agency, by which only a retrospective judgment of incompetence can construe anything else. For it is *never* rightly understood that I act without interest—without what I've conceived of as my best interest at heart—even if it doesn't quite appear so in the moment, which is to say that anyone to whom such act seems contrary to interest is convinced they would do otherwise when put to the same test. And just as well, I could look back on that set of conditions and find myself conspicuously mistaken in the choosing of a profitable course, if not its general method of attainment, surely a more serious offense...

φ

This is not to lay the groundwork for some egoistic practicum, to undermine what makes each disparate animus distinct, but to locate such distinction in the *character* of agency—in that part of the character of one's agency intrinsic to one's consummate enactments of intent. The trick to any moral claim *against* such motivation—against what's thought self-interested *pursuit*—is that one is convinced it isn't *adequately* reasoned; that with proper understanding one would realize that one's wants would best be served by other works. It is to argue that one can't act *as* oneself without first acting *for* oneself; that the variable predicates attributed to agency are only rightly referenced to that intimated crux when they are thought to come about...to *happen* in response to some predictive want...

φ

I believe that you believe that I believe it's in my interest—it's *my intention*, simply put—to give you something...*lead you somewhere*, even if you have no notion where that is just yet. I believe that your belief in my good nature...

φ

By seemingly *arousing* your belief in my good nature, I hope to soon convince you that it's in *your* interest to remain under the spell that that same nature serves to cast. I want you to suppose that when you see our path together—a path, I understand, that's merely *pointed* to as yet—you'll rest easy in the choice...in *having chosen* to take succor in our unremitting concourse for as long as...as long as it takes to...I want to here *expect* that you'll continue in my company—that you've realized

such continuance will continue to *pay off* in opportunities you'd never have the option of rejecting had you failed to pledge your service
to this spasm of a tract. You are, it seems to me, the one for whom
I've made such certainty the prior of conviction—for whom this
gasping wallow of confessions was assembled in the first place—and
so I ask your leave...

φ

Doesn't it *appear* to be shaping up, to be becoming marginally lucid,
admitting that coherence is but a murmur at this point? I turn back,
I turn back once again, I've done so more than once; I turn back to
the front by turning back what I turned into...what I turned into
when...

φ

Such performative locution is a child's trick at most. That each attempt to coalesce this idyll into quiddity has led me to engender one
more supplemental set, to find in the redaction of such dissipated
speech the nature that purportedly contrives it thus—that makes it
glean in excess of the faltering repulse from which it bursts. In short,
I left you stranded at the moment of commencement, the moment
whose primordial ascent I would commence with...

φ

That the character of pain presents...*exemplifies* the range and intimation of all other inner sense I will not argue further; I've made
the point, I think, with more than typical aplomb. What is proved
by the *enactment*, as it were, of such identicals—by this novel understanding of the dearth one's inner takes for its completion, so its
*acting out*—is that one's supplication to the carapace of agency can't
be disengaged from the extension of the agent, from being present in
a world compelled to suffer the vicissitudes of radical doubt...

φ

Yes, I have a surface, I reassured myself, even though its iteration yet proves incomplete. All claims to the contrary serve as equal counter to the fact that one's affective states can be expressed in *any* way, accepting as a consequence that one is only understood the agent of one's affects if one's able to express them...to *conceptualize* expressing them, regardless if one understands that wherewithal as choice. That one finds neither reason nor desire to make evident one's deference to an ecotone—a *syncretism*—of intimated sorrows and delights...

φ

The itch. Itch to continue. I have an itch, that is, to continue. Possession of an absence—of a longing *unfulfilled*—is not difficult to substitute for the presence of some chafing scourge...To continue. Continue the inscription of the character redacted by the cicatrix I've carved out to continue...to move on from the itching to the being soothed...

φ

I have spoken, it appears, of an unspecified discomfiture in order to establish that such diffident arousal is transmissible in some way that is elsewise unexampled; that one can't point to what one feels as though it were extended, but only to that outlying response to inner stimulus, so giving oneself over to a faith in common forms. That I have yet to turn back to the light that turned me back to...to the living of a world in which my skill alone prevails may be annoying, I'm aware—an irritant that nothing but the volte-face I continue here to promise can assuage...

φ

I'm willing to delay further delays by here admitting my delays may appear endless—pointless and so endless—thereby unconcealing my sympathy with your plight. Of course I realize that you still have a choice, but should you have the chance to make it then my apologue has surfaced far too late. I can at least assure you that I'll come back to the border...to the *marginalia* I've claimed a divergence from my path—the fringes of a page whose middle pass I first suggested by suggesting that what's central is at margin, that next to what's at margin must be something like a central span, as the promise of abundance merely wants that its receiver should find repose within his present lack...

φ

You may be such a one, or you may not be, that's *your* problem, but finding myself lost in the excreta of this labyrinth still does nothing to prepare the ground before us—the ground we *share* before us—as much as some next wallow in its verdure may seduce...

φ

All this to make plain that while I labor in description of those many failed attempts to which my former first averred—attempts at once preempted and so equally aroused by such a primeval awakening into the dappled glare—I acknowledge that to take a dive into that whelm of pith would in the end prove inauspicious...*premature*, that is to say, for having yet to fully take account of the embodiment my prurience had only just begun to yield. I had an itch, you may recall, I longed to find its billet, and although my sense of pulp or place was not yet in relation to...to anything in any way at all, I was nonetheless still able to believe that I was in it, still held captive in my placement...

φ

I had an itch I longed to scratch, soon after which I came upon the circumstance I've lived in since—my life as it's conceived *in its continuum*, as it's *come to pass*—but the passages I've left out in between that furtive longing and fulfillment in its act are more than just important; they are essential to the character of my...my *characterization*, I repeat—to the character of the account of my character, insofar as that lapsed egress seems to constitute my character itself...

φ

I had an itch that guaranteed the bulwark of a cosmos—the network of relations that reveal me as extant. The problem, I now realize—or that I realize that I realized at the time—is that my sense of certitude still hadn't found the topos of that very same extension—that I had yet to consummate the *being in* I'd ever thus become by being hence. Once again I feel an explanation is in order, inasmuch as I intend to make my reasoning appear...my mode apparent...*appear to you*, that is, as both a motive and a method—what absent either one would be nonsensical *at best*...

φ

At worst, there may be some of you rebuffed by my diversions, more willing to adjudge this work *designed* to flaunt your ken. That I might seem to *long* for your dismissal of my labors as an idiot's contented preen...

φ

The itch evoked a sense of being fixed within a body, a body that I could presume extended, filling space; it even served to prove, I've proved to *my* satisfaction, the necessity of indwelling to any dwelling in—to being an entelechy *endowed* with such a character, with what appears to measure up as agency, or...

φ

90

What was missing when I left off this summation of my exploits—an absence made apparent...*given credence* by my having taken steps to start again—was what that...what that was that I was *filling in* by such immersion; what the nature of my placement in a world and in a body...

φ

Absent was the *suchness*—the *default*—of that alightment, despite its claim to having been discerned within a pose, and equally the fact that all discrete discernment *of* it had gone quite as far as it could...

φ

The itch I had, you see, appeared to drift about my torso, with nary a determinable moment in one place; the itch conveyed my carcass and its surface to presentiment—the focus of the ego that, in essence, I've been since. Or has become me. To the ego I've become by its having become me...

φ

It was not the sort of itch I could conceive a way of tracing, a concentrated quantum to consolidate the sense. It's not that it appeared to move before I could attend it—that it moved faster than I could, or than I did; it was more like...I don't know...swimming in a tonic whose sole nature was vexation—was prurience at every point at which it touched my...

φ

Imagine there's a pustule or a membrane on the surface of what otherwise delineates one's terminus as *bound*—and at that very instant finding what one's focussed *on* dispersed to countless distal plains; imagine oneself pricked with pins immeasurably miniscule, that at each point one can make *out* another pushing in. Where, in such an overload of incongruent stimulus, would it even be *possible* to locate one's awareness—to designate the character of consciousness thus crazed? How could one secure a stable posture of surveillance, to designate that incubating torpor as *domain*...

φ

Such an image in the mind's eye...well, you can see by the difficulty of conjuring such an image in the mind's eye that merely *trying* to describe it is to have one's mind deranged. But in what sense, you'd like to ask, could I make out derangement from the wash of sensibilities I've cast as such an ordered kind, a classed array? And if you'd like to, I suppose, then I ought here suppose you have...

φ

I'm trying to convey the sense that...how to put it...if your intellect is stratified—put in its place and order—then imagine the abstraction of that order from its range, or maybe one should think of it the other way around...Try to disengage the binding predicate of agency—the binding that was *acting* as the predicate of agency, for lack of any other...any more precise...And what do you have. But wait. The problem...the problem with such summary *description* of the problem lies in the very nature of this adventitious dodge, that if I am to ask you to imagine the derangement of the idiom by which such image is to be, for first and last, *arranged*...

φ

I don't know where to go. How discern digression without avenue to stray from? Difference without synchrony to mark the turn? How conceive a world whose one discriminating feature is its inconceivability? Its having been removed from any measurable scale? There is no point. Imagine there's no point—and that's the point. The set of sets only defined as members of themselves...

φ

I claim I have an itch, suggesting I would like to scratch it. All that you can know...can at your best *assume* is that my state of irritation bears resemblance to what *you* feel when you're similarly poised. I try to illustrate, when I can gather up the gumption, that this is where the itch is—where it was, after its parting—that I've determined where to strike by *some* form of surveil, but the stimulus through which it's come to stimulate my interest is not thereby depicted, nor is such depiction really relevant to the cure...

φ

I may have been impaled by thorn or slathered with some toxic ointment, but I might just as well have no pretension to know cause; it is as I perceive it—set beneath the peel or on it—and I only seek its origin as a secondary aim. This, again, is neither faith nor practicable certainty; it doesn't matter that you grasp *exactly* what I've said, but I assume you do, and such assumption—as likely to prove false of any single in the crowd—here takes on the posture of a premise, of a *given*; of that for which I need set forth no precedent at all...

φ

This, it seems quite plain, is still most commonly the frame of any itch presumed transmissible in name or made the referent of some condign inebriant or corrosive balm, requiring one understand the stimulus as singular all across the field of moments over which one feels its brand, even if in retrospect it reads but one of some. Such determination may necessitate a greater...a more broadly *scavenged* cull, but however that discretely self-identical apportioning is purposed—whether clear to that who suffers its indelible effects or to some gallant quidnunc who attempts to help reduce its pulse or vitiate its thrum—each event described as such a member must be singular, by virtue of the limits of the limner as a source. The limits of all diegetic artifice...

φ

It soon appears *remarkable*, I'm sure you'll soon agree, that this sort of associative reasoning is possible...is *com*possible with a feeling while it's given, while it's felt; that one can come to understand some stimulus as *portion*, as part within a total whose distinction as a *limit* is obscure. It is, as such, *provocative* because it claims no datum, only the assumption of a knowledge that, with prodding, will prove true, if not yet real—a courtesan who won't yield to her paramour's caresses without some declaration of intent...

φ

It only scans as willful insofar as what inscribes it as disease or mere condition—as a momentary misery of unknown cause or a state of retribution for some common sin—is the fact that by the gleaning of its predicable particulars the same referent is...is referred to, is *envisioned*; a bond that's only thought removed when all that stands within it can be understood...*presumed*, that is, detached, if not withdrawn...

φ

I say I have an itch, the aspiration to abrade it, and whether I've determined that some irritant is present or have only the sensation in itself to give me pause, I can do so, I can do it—and so I have unwittingly assumed a cause outside me, a reason why what's in me...what's *of* me is no longer mine in purpose *or* in will...

φ

I want to scrape that tender rot with rancor and debasement—the same that I'd apply to any similar duress—and for the purpose of revealing my impalpable environs such a singular displacement of my agency outside me—outside me, so against me—ought be a suitable intent. I'd find my place, I'd take my marks, by finding place upon me—a field that is extended as an aggregative husk—and thereby make the first move towards assembling an image...a representative *abstraction* of said reign over a world at once extended and...

φ

I would thrust into the open, I would open to the clear. This terminal reprise of the importance of that pinprick would allow me to continue with describing its return, now bolstered with full certainty of having lead you to it, of having first and foremost thought to bring you up to speed. Up to *full* speed, the breakneck pace of my adventures...

φ

The problem that afflicts me now, I'm somewhat sad to tell, has nothing to do with my belief in your perverse proclivities or your simpering avowals of impassioned zeal. Instead, it puts in question only *my* crass ingenuity; my own dissimulation of conditions that might well have proved sufficient for my forthcoming deliverance had they ever come to pass, but they just didn't, as it turns out—as it turns out the solution to my quandary was not found in the apportioning of body parts and irritants in turn...

φ

If I had had an itch of this most sanative variety, a tender spot whose local...whose *locality* could be at once determined and addressed, disclosing to the prurient compendium it vexes—none other than your beggarly bellwether on this path—the position of some portion of that body in relation to another...to *any* other similarly proffered as extant, then surely I could move on, as I have...as I *once did*, back when I felt neither need to right your understanding of the source and stimulation of my first...my allegedly *primordial* escape nor reason to expect some wary second to attain this breach position in the transit from conjecture to account. Not to say I wouldn't find an ease in doing just so. I'd be perfectly happy to leave you in a certitude I *know* is mistaken if I believed its only consequence would be that lapsed conceit; if, that is, some like default in *my* advance towards certainty would not be a near certain effect...

φ

I'm not trying to suggest I *didn't* have an itch, or long to scratch it, but that I was unable to achieve that lofty aim...I have spoken rather broadly of the auspices evoked when one groups disparate stimuli into some one condition, an exploit instantly encompassing each inkling of intellect thought *self*. And in—or *during*—such account it has likewise occurred to me that every disparate member of a set need be thought singular, insofar as it's distinguished as in part distinct at all. If it were only so under the circumstance that brought on this recital we'd be fine; needless to say, it was not. Needless for the fact that if it were I'd have refrained from further discourse on the matter—*we'd all be fine*, I say again, and so would want for no delay—in favor of progressing towards...progressing towards progressing...

φ

While much of this *pre*liminary account seems irrefutable—or nearly so, that is, when it's assembled as a proof—the claim on which the explanation turns is still a species of dissemblance; the *interval* through which I first professed the seeming placement of the itch at just one point...at any one point in particular, in series or as some culmination of effects, was neither felt nor understood as happening that instant, which is to say as that one instant passed...

φ

I did not feel an itch, a single itch, at any moment; I felt some countless many on the surface and at core. I felt what I'd describe as a *plu-*

*rality* of portents, and yet could differentiate no one at any turn. Not at any point, nor any multiple insertion, but all at once at each transparent tickle of a pang—every plicate portion of the space in which I dwelled...from which I gathered...

φ

Every infinite extension is divided...is *divisible* when taken as a whole made up of parts and parted members, of portions and apportionings of portions each in turn...

φ

What I felt was not a singular, nor a succession of singulars, but a singular immersion in a series...

φ

Just at that one moment I could not conceive a singular—a singular that would succeed in proving its *extent*—and for the length of time that I should be transfixed within it...beside it...against it—that I was not as *other else again*, immured in place—I realized there was nothing to be done with that congeries but relinquish all my efforts to construe it as a *total*, the act of supplication that compelled me to this stance...

φ

It should be clear by now that what I'm doing is not easy, and so for reasons soon to be regarded...*employed* to grease the scabrous palm of the matter at hand; that while I can amuse myself by speaking in the singular...*of* the singular sensation that fields selfdom at its bourne, I'm nonetheless unable to describe the itch *as* singular, as *happening* in its own place, in its own time ...

φ

I could not find a way to fix the field of the sensation—to mark off the *immurement* of the sense—while knowing that possessing it was suitable to gather what I knew...what I *hoped* would someday come to seem a place to place the corpus that I'm placed in...

φ

I was, it seemed, *all* itch, without a post to find my person—any *portion* of my person—in the whole towards which such putative apportioning alludes, let alone a sense of how to make my way from *noticing* that prurience to some species of appeasement, to use some part part of the world to mitigate the strain. All I need, I thought, is some small part spared the immersion...

φ

How...how...I was going to say unnerving, but I haven't shown myself to be sufficiently caparisoned with nerves to suffer so; how endlessly *confusing*, even as the stimulus that caused that wan arousal served to specify my outline, so to constitute my frame. *A* frame, I should say, for that it was all mine was not yet certain. I knew that what I was did not stall at some inference of an aggregated bound, that sense itself extending past the frontage of what nonetheless appeared my sole concern...

φ

I was *all* itch, all itch alone, at surface and at middle, a node of idle longing at the center of the world. Could I but think of one part...any one part in particular—could I concern myself with only one such finite span—then I could use that isolated part, or one beside it...A part *cut off* could ready me to locate my surrender, allowing some odd piece to grind against the wayward collop where the itch seemed to disclose its place, if not, as such, abide...

φ

Just the thought of some relief proved some relief—provided *comfort*—even as I had no way to bring that thought to act. But how, I asked myself, is the *idea* of this remediable torment still at variance with the stimulus that cordons me within such expectation—the bloat from which that incidental affect is transfixed? It's obvious that separating part from any parcel implies an *intuition* of totality—of what one might distinguish as a totalizing cause—so what to do to properly denominate that dissonance, that schism thought as singular, but still within...

φ

I may well understand myself as one made up of pieces—as some inferred assemblage of particulars, that is—and still think that the primary distinction of importance is not within that unity but marked off by its difference from the set of things extrinsic—things that can't be reckoned part of that whose fractured reckoning repels towards some next partage of the whole. And even as I image that dissevering of resources—as I notice that I'm noticing but some *share* of the view—I'm equally aware of that which nonetheless escapes me—lo those many sensitivities that make any wholeness possible by acting as the drab expanse from which its bounds are hewn...

φ

If I understand anything, if I'm able to know anything...

φ

It seems to me that when I have the sense I'm sensing anything—of being posed assessor of my quickening terrain—I'm sensing that to which no sense of notice has been granted—*towards* which no eager surfeit of attention has been turned. That even as I may only devote some measly portion of my resources—my *attentional* resources—to sense taken *in toto*, the rest, by definition, remains an equal substance, no less than that extrinsic trove from which it was expelled...

φ

If I can't hope to *extricate* my culpable receptors—those bits of my extension on which world acts as a goad—then my attention to some swaddled pittance of that gathering of pricks and their responses amounts to little more than one small part within the total, the intimated aggregate of some tumescent whole. And if this is indeed the score, one can't *but* want to know, then what is it that differs that disbursement from submergence in the total of all berths that gives us impetus, so spurs us to...

φ

Perhaps I am alone in being made uneasy; we need not *feel* the same for us to share a common cause. We need not feel we share a common cause for us to do so, or have our disparate ends set in shared bounds...

φ

It may be true that we share cause that *neither* of us knows of, or that either can claim knowledge of without common consent. Similarly, each of us may claim a common cause and be mistaken—a cause that may hold true for only some when it's thought out. My point is that the cause I'd like to think we have together—that's understood as common to us both in this regard—beguiles us to supervene the evidence of its veracity—to make duly irrelevant your knowledge of it as a truth or falsehood or at all...

φ

I am, I thought, intractably immersed in my sensations, although they seem to differ from one passage to the next, and within every moment that I seem to be a selfdom thus embodied...thus *constructed,*

I understand but part of the totality that *mounts* me on the head of this pinpoint escarpment by excluding some...some *infinite* remainder of that crushing cull, that whelming heap, dissevering myself from such extension beyond limit in the service of the marginal discernment of the rest...

φ

How can I sequester some mere portion of my notice when even as that pretermission happens I'm subjected to an utterly unhindered drift? What befalls that hastily redacted understanding when it can't play a role in what it constitutes—the attention *to attention* that it constitutes—beyond which we're denied all further access to...

φ

And even if we grant as *given* such a parted prime, what is that prime but some new whole, against which one still struggles to secure a further part? Is not each concatenated unity of stimulus another intimation of the portion it exempts, so contriving the most liberally inclusive sense of sensing as a surreptitious partisan within an unknown...what appears as an *unknowable* expanse? Why not apply the same restrictive standards of discernment to every part construed as whole, as fenced off span? Why accept as breach that part of parting that...

φ

Just as I conceive of every sense set in its total—a whole I can't discern but for its ever dreamed refute—so can every portion understood *as* such a total seem a reference and inversion of another severed part. Every total is a part, and every part a total, and each avers the other without possible...without the *possibility* of end, of ending somewhere...

φ

Whatever where that finds its next presumption of a bound by thus referring to some wherever whose *what* has not been found will follow that same infinite reversion of a line—a whole that's been partitioned into parts made wholes partitioned...

φ

Take any one sensation that's been excised from its correlates—that's specified as whole by its discernment as a part; of all my sensitivities aroused and manumitted, I can only ever manage to distinguish some allotment as it ciphers my subsistence in a world always elided, always *to come*...

φ

I feel upon an elbow, say, some bland excoriation, a squamous patch that itches all across the rigid join; it does not spread beyond the edge of forearm or of bicep, but still it seems continuous with the wallow of relations that it theorizes, a sense that covers but a few square inches, nothing more. Is it possible for me to be attendant to the impulse as it travels—as it *pains* me—all across that withered span? Where is the itch, the scab, the molt of the abraded? All in the same place, but just how far does it extend? How much less of an infinity for being set within a smaller sum...

φ

The problem is that within every length that can be parted—whether seen as an extension into scale or over term—one can as well identify an equal to its outside, as no such endless portion can be greater than or lesser to...to any other anywhere, without consideration of the margins that inscribe it, so that it assumes...

φ

Once again, the measure of the *quantity* is frivolous; no difference *need* be thought in *all* sense different or in *any* sense the same. To note the state of some part as the irritant awakes me, to *have* to turn my mind to that one part and that alone, is to explicate said itch by what it forces on me, what it requires *of* me if I hope to let it go. Let it revert—let it *assemble*—into the creeping mire from which everything...from which everything I'm mired in...

φ

You may find the postponement of an adequate resumption of my life within the world to be quite droll, that all my stores should be depleted in the mere act of distinguishing some mere attempt to act, but even so that *mere* is a return to where I started, when I could find no method to find out anything else. Would that we could be compelled to stake our first philosophies...to stake *out* something like this fretful claim as first philosophy...

φ

I suppose it is my purpose to endure such inculcation—to begin your search in earnest by displaying mine in kind...as of a kind with what it asks of its seductive eavesdroppers before they can *drop in* to take account of this surmise. It's not that I'd expect you to go further, or that I'll even have the chance to claim it's happened so; it's an *organizing* principle that I could have abandoned...could just as well and readily refuse to bring to bear upon the tattered confines of my tale, but I still see in its advancement a result that can harm no one—that can *only* prove of benefit, would that it should come into the world just as I've planned...

φ

That I discern a tingle on the margins of my trunk is hardly notable; that I should understand that stroke as other than...*irreducible to* the whole in which it plays but some small part—well, I ask you, what other coextensive mode of stimulus is not equally distinguished from its inferential purview? And is there any way to cease that portioning of thetic rot...

φ

The answer goes on endlessly, without resolve. It's not that I would give up, given my druthers—that the want of explanation has ever... *will* ever stop me in my efforts to contribute some embellishment to this distrait accord—but that I do not need such satisfaction to move forward...to move back to the place that I moved on from when...

φ

I *am* engaged in such attempts at progress, it seems clear, for all my blithe endeavors to present a wholly paralytic pose. I've left behind—or *cast aside*—all trace of my surroundings, the scene that I was in when I began this reprimand—the pain in neck, the crook in back, the elbows well upbraided as they press the plastic pine—in order to devote myself...to turn all my attentions to the feeling of *dis*ease at the reprisal of my easement...my drift into...

φ

The solace I'm proposing is not found in new concern, but in realizing my sense of inner turmoil is not merely ineffectual, but without *any* effect. As such, I continue with these turns in the redundancy of having my attention *never* set upon the whole; I won't turn my attention to the whole it still inclines towards, as it appears such notice is *itself* what differentiates each parting from what's altogether part...

φ

Every turning to the whole that I've contrived a predicate of some set that's inscrutable for being thought complete—the all-at-once *completed* cull in which that very turning plays...in which each one distinguished from all others plays a part...Every *inclination* of awareness towards a one descries another one within it, and so on to an infinite that can't bear drawing out...

φ

That the regress first divulged by finding part in every whole should equally confound one's seeing every whole as part—as *whole* part in which ever smaller parts can be discerned—should no longer abash. There is a sort of force set at the nexus of one's cognizance that gives the next priority...the next *previous* priority to some part in particular; somehow some one part presents the exigence of exiting the regress of awareness before that same awareness seems to happen— so to *take effect*—and what that is, or where it's sourced...what the source of that...that singular installed at the horizon...

φ

All of which does little to impart my sense of urgency—or proffer a description of my forthcoming escape. Clearly, you must realize I'm no longer in the throes of that impassive apoplexy; that I can't now elucidate my paralysis by reference to...*by relating* my imprisonment in prurience, that is, for having brought you this far towards a comprehensive chronicle of my plight...

φ

I've spoken of it passing, of having lived a life up to this...this moment that's not in it, and that with an attention to detail doomed to convince all those who'd take me at my word of the sincerity of the gest. Even if the claim proves a dissemblance some time hence, you can be sure I'll have disposed of the conundrum in a manner that...You can be assured that either I was guilty of exaggerating the extent of my difficulties in the first place or that I've found a way to remedy a sickness whose depths and protestations I have hardly made coherent in the last; in either case, the first or last—in any case at all, I say—it's clear...it *must* be clear *by now* that I have since escaped that fate, or at the least delayed...

φ

With respect to which the mere act of description ought prove adequately tempting to succor your belief in such emergence—emergence from a scene whose very indescribability seems to constitute its nature as a trap. All I need do now, I thought, is try to notice something...something and not everything...something so distant from intimating everything to stop at the topography of being thus—and only thus—extant...

φ

Alas, if I could only pluck the angles of my amplitude from the similarly overwrought dimensions of the world, a world I'd never doubted for a moment was describable as limitless—as wholly *in*describable when taken as a whole—then I would find my way out of this artifice of absence, the torpor of this incoherent vale. Not knowing *what* it was or where I was within it didn't give me reason to doubt *that* it was *as such*; to the contrary, the intransigence of that sensitivity to the absence of all other sensitivities made requisite a referent for that whole to fill, to fill that hole, to fill...

φ

If I could but *describe* the pose I knew I could escape it, that I could thereby mollify the discontent of finding myself in it for a time. The problem was that any intimation of the total first required the discernment—so the *making out*—of some whit deemed its centerpiece, its accidental *axis*; a pivot point whose distance from the sense of sensing everything would equally allow the sense of mise-en-scene in part...

φ

106

I need only discern, I thought, some fraction of the world to see my desolation in it—as perfectly within it—but marking off the distance from that ideal with such excruciating constancy was getting me nowhere; was *leaving* me nowhere, which is precisely the location I was trying...I was hoping soon to *realize* that I'd managed to relinquish, to *depart*...

φ

The practice of the limner is difficult enough without placing the burden of such manumission on it—expecting the transcendence of conditions only extant once the action of discharging them is met. This is only to take note of the modality made manifest by noticing one's taking note of anything at all, a scene at once made absent by suppression of that deictic drive—of the drive *or* the activity said drive would bring about...

φ

I may well be aware a certain ambit is discomfiting—I may find I'm discomfited when subject to the view—but having at the ready no clear method of discernment still have no idea how *not* to rest within it for a time; how to *understand* myself as something more than immanent, in excess of...of that set that's inscribed by my reflexive comprehension, by that its members illustrate the limits of my heft. The paradox of knowing *that* there is without quite knowing *what* there is—if it constitutes a paradox, properly thought—is what, in general terms, collates the taint and tone of indecision that living at the mercy of such an abstract membership effects...

φ

And perhaps it's not. A paradox, that is. Perhaps it does not quite comprise a circumstance that contradicts *itself* so much as it suggests such contradiction in the actor—the actor who has nonetheless discerned it as a *lapse*. Naturally, you say, it may not be what you expected—what you've presumed the *standard* of such knowing in its place. You thought that you'd awake with some idea of where you'd landed, and so conceive a way of knowing *some* part...some *trifling* part, even, of what within that circumstance contrives the source and character of stimulus...

φ

Let me grant your terms, then, and be done with it—but first I must know this. Or this I must point out. First I must admit I don't know this. This that I'm about to ask. Or it's answer, rather. First the question, then the answer—so, it seems to me, is how it works, even when the answer is a *lack*. How I *expect* it to work, whether or not in *this* instance that's what it does, or how it will do when...

φ

In this form, as the former, is there really any reason to expect my thwarted foresight to prove out the conditions that contrived it thus? To believe that such expectancy portends what ought to be, and if so that this *ought* will soon surrender to the fact of its adherence to said proof? As though there were another choice, but still...

φ

I want that I should know something—that I should have the skill to *represent* it—because my *having done so* has marked progress in the past. I want to progress further in...in my perturbed progressions, whatever I have come to think they are, or will be next—whatever they have come to *seem*, at least. *This*—and this *alone*—I will accept...

φ

If nothing else I want to say I know what drives me forward—and so in turn exalt it as felicitous response. Even when it's evidenced by what its daft betokener *inducts*, such expectation has little to do—need not have *anything* to do, whether it has a little or a lot—with one's present condition, or with the sense of world thus offered up...

φ

That I want to know more than I do, and have reason to expect I will, still doesn't make it possible—prove it can ever happen, let alone will happen soon. In this instance I think I've shown—we've shown, that is, *together*—that there is *something* knowable, no matter *what* it's name; something that's not presently depicted in this missive, but nonetheless that could have been, could still...

φ

No doubt it has occurred to you that I may well be lying, and as such be describing the internal life of one who I have never...whose thoughts and pains are not my own—have not slipped the inertia I've described myself *within*. Many failed attempts, and all that...

φ

And if the prospect troubles you, then let me ask you this; what difference would it make *to you* if I were nothing *but* the affectation of a voice? Would this confession seem less true for having been made up? And what could any truth portend that such dissemblance can't? Or *doesn't*? Might not this incantation seem as much of an excursus—just as pointless as a missive, as a reason to speak *out*—absent any reference to the truth of the events that it narrates? If you've met me even halfway—read every other word, or every third—you have your answer. You have, that is, *accepted* the collateral effects of taking in my testament while it still constitutes a null set, whether evidenced by some show of indelible esteem or by some subtle demonstration of a singularly inner state. As to the stupefying character of all those indiscernibles into which I had awaked...I once awoke...

φ

The fact that I had proved the fact that there was there an extant that had been at last aroused, if not forsook—*to* which I'd been forsaken, if not yet aroused—appears to me the linchpin—so the *mainstay*—of the argument. Of the disquisition argued, or given pride of access to the pretense of a voice. To *this* voice, as a vow, having no path to mete another—another that is not at once supposed to be the same...

φ

I may have yet supposed what it would be...what I would *find* when I awoke to find it absent—to find what I'd supposed my given knowledge *of* it absent—but that is not, you may recall, the course by which I came to think that immanent extension proved extant; it had nothing to do with it, admitting just the same that this intractable expectancy may well have played some role in the concealment of an independent proof...

φ

Having realized there was something there to know, I thought that I need surely...need must prove that such unknown was knowable, or knowing it was knowable that it was somehow knowable to *me*, in place and form...

φ

It seemed emergent at the time—a dire situation, if I haven't made it clear—but seeing now in retrospect that I would soon escape it, in retrospect it doesn't really seem so bad at all. I still felt—*can* still feel—the pain and consternation of that generalized uncertainty, all with an intensity it's difficult to tell. I could manage to do just so, but not without great difficulty, and it doesn't seem to justify the interval it bodes. If I could do it with great difficulty but also *in an instant,* some mere interlude…

φ

In this form of endeavor, I've come to understand, the measure of difficulty is in direct proportion to the length of term. I could say I've had problems finding methods of conveyance, and the claim would garner adequate support, but if that trouble should result in some propulsive brevity when my labors have been birthed into this bloviating stint, then the difficulty would rest solely in *that* practice—in *myself* and not another—and so appear extrinsic to the object of the query, which is what…which is the *essence* of the trouble that I'm trying to…

φ

It's difficult to convey my difficulty in…in having once *attempted* to convey, at *some* point in the past—some point at least not present… not *presently* my state of grace—the depth of the discomfiture I felt when in that moment—an effort only clarified by gazing back upon it from the prospect of the promontory slope. It's difficult to convey the difficulty of conveying, as indexed by the present germination of attempts, pursued over what must appear…what must appear *to you* as an interminable expanse…

φ

It's difficult to convey the nature of the pain, and that not for the inadequacy of my faculties of conveyance, but the character of the pain itself. As though one could conceive emancipation from one's character—could *find*, that is, one's character in avoidance of one's character…

φ

Mercifully said character has proved worthless to my story—which is not to claim it would prove so to unrelated ends. Indeed, this is an obstacle we've already encountered, a crude way to remind you of the pain that my endeavors to elucidate the pain have since achieved... have *bodied forth*, as though it were the only discrete characterization of such inner life...

φ

I won't linger in the making of such a futile point. And why, perchance, would this point prove so eminently pointless, when so many other tangents have impelled me in good stead? Do I have cause *but* for such peripheral excursus, a palsied retrogression to the voided fray? This appears to be the very substance of the matter, and for bringing it to my attention you have my eternal thanks. As though you could be satisfied with any form of gratitude. As though you were the one who brought this *on yourself*...

φ

That this is not the way our shared exigency transpired has not escaped me; my voice is my voice, and it belongs to no one else. In principle, this vestige of a personhood discarded is always a determinant—this voice, that is, is *personal*, a keening singularity that's mustered in the service of a singular pursuit. That so much of what I've done should seem irrelevant...unrelated to...to so much else I've done in the same incidental stroke...

φ

The irrelevance of *some* of what I've done to a description...a *portrayal* of *everything* I've done to reach those same discrepant ends is no concern of yours...of *ours*, eliding the penultimate to make of every second a plurality of primaries, of...

φ

In one's attempts to extirpate the figure of the speaker by a riffle through the spoken one must *first* suppose that every iteration of that voice is just and only that, is of *itself* and not another; that even if one can't decline...*deny* the jilted portent of such intimate alterity, it's nonetheless an alter that will serve its quick attendant as a shadow of the singular who speaks...

φ

Should I tell you that just now, just at the first last diacritical, I resumed this recitation with the notion of completing the reprisal of that fabulist who's since vacated this pen, you still would have no refuge but in such a generous singular—a *moment* in the sweeping prosecution of the same delinquent ends. And *to* me, as you've gathered from my musings hitherto, you can only seem a corollary selfdom, which is to say a singular disguised by some new desiccant or interest at each bar. Each of you is only as the one to whom I'm speaking...*for the sake* of whose attention I remain, sincerely yours...

φ

The irrelevance of my pain to its transcendence is irrelevant to the question of the relevance of a *description* of my pain to its transcendence, itself entirely irrelevant to the relevance of the transcendence of my pain to the return—which I will soon not fail to privilege...to *purpose* in the name of...of something...of that thing still unnamed, still *coming on*—to that sense of dominion...of *describable* dominion I've long alleged the terminus of this fawning disport...

φ

It's not that either my discomfort as I felt it then or a description of it now, now that I've left it...now it's left me...I don't know...That a description of my pain now that it's finished or my pain itself would be inconsequential to *all* purposes, distant or implied, or that either would prove apropos of anything or nothing, given the right circumstance—what seems the *proper* circumstance to consummate the ruddy wash of paper over pen...

φ

Nor is it that there's *nothing* one can say of such an unresolved vexation, announcing its importance to a chronicle of...of the feeling of it when it was imbued; instead I'd have you understand my zealotry in finding a solution to the frenzied feint that ancillary anguish manifests only in part—a *symptom*, and not a cause...

φ

If it remained my wont to *represent* that agitation, I'd have no option but to name the consonance required of me by it—by the experience *of* it—but this erratic posture leaves me no such leg to stand on, as it were. The integrity of my inertia came promptly on the heels of having lived a life unburdened by such tangible design, for having yet to think myself as animate in the first place—as being in a body in a world...

φ

No lithic form or filigree is posed as paralytic because it is assumed to be its only proper mode; neither is a megrim or caprice conceived as stagnant, even if its referent is not found within the world. One may have ideas, that is, just as one has limbs, but the motility of one's eidetic members is not surfaced, not *extended*; it reflects a certain fluid state of flex and elasticity, a comfort in conforming to new predicates—or predicates of predicates...

φ

Likewise one's appendages may welcome ruddy carbuncles or take on something like a second skin, but such addition...such *acceptance*, even, of what otherwise appears a toxic strain has nothing at all to do with one's innate adaptability, the fulfillment of the impulse that the seizure countermands. Such satiated stock is always subject to my bounding sense of agency...my sense of bounding agency, instruments whose character is only made potentia when it's mustered against stasis...against standing as an object, as...

φ

Inertia fairly intimates the world as it appears—the thing fit to its present form, its will to stay the same. Some *tendency*, that is, against the volatile surge distinguishes the set that it invariably contrives— that it contrives the set of things invariably contrived—by which any decisive move against formal discernment...against the *form discerned* is an exertion, thus a stimulus; constitutes an act against the being in—the *stillness*—of the same...

φ

So the inward glance that frames identity *as such*—the equivalence of being...of *beings* with themselves—is always a surrender to inaction—to *inertia*—without which one would be denied all claim to phase or mode. Things that move achieve that state by ceding to an outside, a difference manumitted from inertia *by* inertia, so by the refusal to keep keeping up the change...

φ

If one conceives of being in...of being in *or* as a given form as an activity, then only an acquittal of such comprehensive stasis can transcend one's acquiescence to eidetic presentation in the world. And what does such exemption look like when it happens? What need one do to manifest the absence of all doing—to take one's stance against being identical *to oneself*...

φ

Persistency endues a sort of quitclaim to putrescence, a final transformation into nothing like...nothing like or unlike, either way. Such replete abandon—such unqualified inertia—is the only real constraint, so the only active answer, to the torpid metaphysics of all bearing, bearing all...

φ

Or maybe I'm confusing the idea with what it names. When is one's conception of the thing set in its thingness exactly as that thing itself appears? Can one discern those traits that differentiate an object without distinguishing the predicates that make of each such predicate an object in its turn? And does not every predicate discerned as some like object shed the taint of variation as it courses through the compound tropes to which it's been adjoined—*despite* being identical to itself? A vector down, a sloughing stain...

φ

And with each new individual that the set must now subsume is it not newly conceived...newly *extended*, an endless iteration of mutations and accords? And yet...but still...and yet I still require that the change in state or nature I require hold within it some odd kernel of the state that came before; that such a change in nature is not as a *denaturing*...takes with it *some* particulate of what it supersedes, a glacial crawl that can't help but transport the turf it scours...

φ

This is going nowhere. What would you have me do. Again my odd predicament in *describing* my predicament describes my predicament with far greater accuracy than the description of my predicament *as* predicament has done. It *parallels*, that is, that same paralysis of order...no...that paralysis that rests between those orders of disorder that identify all consort in this carnal fen...

φ

Anyone who's lived within a world—so anyone towards whom my servile speechifying aims—knows that I'm right. You may not *know* you know, but that's where I come in. How, after all, can one adduce a claim as true only for those who've had the good fortune of receiving it, of granting it as given, as a premise proved? We may have taken different paths to reach the same conclusions, but if those paths are equal to the name of universal, then each—both yours *and* mine—will yield equivalent results. We may not *feel* the same way at departure or arrival, but that can't matter. That you should now be forced to sanction *my* dreamed universals...

φ

There is reason to believe, if nothing else is clear—or has *become* so as we slither towards to the finish of this précis, a pass you can be sure is coming soon—that seeing my peculiar verve directed towards your betterment will better you in ways still unintended, even if its object is not rendered by its causatum or mentioned hitherto. It's obvious that *I* would like to think it so, at any rate, and should you claim my thinking a demonstrable mistake, one might be led to understand there's something to be learned from such objection... from watching such objectionable *discourse* meet its end. You may *want* to think you can avoid your destination, but when avoidance is your destiny...

φ

So many times I've given up, this first of all my many failed attempts notwithstanding. I have given up so many times, though in all honesty I must admit that this time is the first, the very first. If you've ever tried your hand at such a comprehensive apologue you won't be the least astonished to find this sort of obstacle—so the promise of its *rout*—put in your path, proclaiming against interest that your *next* failure to fail will leave behind no trace of the deceit...

φ

Why not. Take your time. Why rush to the gallows when you know that they'll be burning down the jail. If my position seems obscure, then you're right there, right where you need be to accept it when it comes around again. If I'm to tell you anything—and clearly I think I *have*—then it comes at the expense of my *own* specificity, producing little more than some crude picture of the world it seems we share...

φ

It's an odd device, I'll grant you. In making these attempts to vault the quizzical inertia of my suppliance to action—*to having something happen*, in consequence of what amounts to chasing my own tail—I've given too much credit to the gifts of my admirers—whoever they may represent, if not someday reveal—resulting in a largely inconspicuous return to prior minimum...

φ

Should the wary supplication that's compelled you to this juncture have begun to feel like servitude, then consider yourself released. You may come away from our acquaintanceship with little else; if it proves true—if it *proves out*—I'll count myself among the few endowed to offer such exemption...to *perform* it, if you will, with neither warrant nor rebuke, an actor who finds wherewithal to end the play before the curtains rise. An actor who seeks purchase—not in preen and ostentation—but in tearing down the theater from the wings...

φ

But I'm not there yet. Or you're not. We're not there *together*, it should be obvious by now, but just who sets the stage, and who plays player...One cannot merely *ask* for understanding and expect to be transformed. Perhaps such pained petition has resulted from such vatic transformation *having happened*—that one should come to understand there's something not yet understood, and understanding thus should soon redress the cleft by...by closing it, accepting that a failure to do just so would make permanent an injury that same orison alleges to have healed...

φ

I think it's fair to think I've been of service, if only to myself; that I've shed a little light on the affliction that provoked me, a scene I can't imagine any other voice sustaining with such ease of will. I couldn't have made due with the inertia I was promised...I was *ceded* by the ongoing disaster of my time, and that sense of undoing...of my doing *against* undoing as a matter not of choice but of redundancy...that's not it...but of *necessity* has been long since foreshadowed by this most general sketch of my...

φ

Perhaps I have been lucky in achieving my vocation by coercion, for having then and there—in parsing out the stratagems within which I was stranded at the start of this, my seeming stand—been forced to the retreat. Perhaps given the chance I would have lived as you have, in the affable confusion of thinking my thoughts through. Judge for yourself. Or rather, I'm still struggling to inculcate a judgment that is *not* yours—that is not what *you* have chosen; to formulate the same dissatisfaction that I've come to live myself. I want to here oblige you to make out the world as I do—a vision of the absence into which I've been repulsed; to give you ample reason to pursue the ends that I have, and by the same arousal of your formerly unknown finesse make that sloth appear not only justice, but requite...

φ

Why else would one bother with such abject reportage—such claim to claim and story, to a claim that's never made? Why else but in service to some postured pedagogy make a journey—an *adventure*—of such floundering accord? No standard of amusement is worth framing as a purpose—I have openly refused all bids to win you by such vim. I have even forgone efforts to portray myself as admirable, or convince you that I have *your* interest at heart...

φ

It is for others to make light of your monotony, your boredom; of your aching to find place, and so a placement...others to *distract* you from what bothers you the most. What I *assume* supports your manifestly apt frustrations for having found myself inscribed by just such an abuse—our least common denominator, if I've got it right. The truth of our predicament is our least common denominator, by which I hope to calculate the union of our contrary...what may have at one time appeared our differences in kind, our least pursuit...

φ

And even these attempts to win your favor—the convivial release from lack, from bathos and distrust—aren't able to distract us, to make light of the revenant that queers our sense of being whole...the wholeness of our senses, of our *being sense*. Any sort of appetence one chances as dispositive—even that it should take on the savor of a need—is only rightly understood as requisite—as *dictum*—by reference to some previous awareness of awareness as a bracket around absence, an absence which said want presumes discovered, if not precisely mapped out from the start of the next...

φ

That you've made it here at all is ample proof. I will not claim it demonstrates your benevolence or your penury, but in each instance you are, by definition, who I want. It's possible that you find my demeanor entertaining—I can at least *imagine* such repose, on second thought—but this, too, bears witness to your difference from the many feckless ruminants I've lost over this sojourn, or those who till their dying day would not commit to start. Or just plain *do* so; there have been false commitments...

φ

My hope is to convince you our adventure is *in common*—that we've embarked together on a path whose end is clear—and to do so, I might add, by first describing...first *delivering* the monody of vows and incantations that will constitute its reach across the great divide...

φ

If the interest I've exacted still appears to you excessive, now that you've faced the peril of avoiding its increase—well, I here commend you, you have more than made your point. I'm not saying you're right, mind you, but that it would be wrong for you to have conjectured otherwise, even as I know that no such abstract motivation will ever serve to designate my index of contrary intents...

φ

I think you'll find that this is my peremptory distinction, if indeed you're looking for my difference from the pack—that my sense of vocation or of vision is not purposed by attempts to lead you slantwise, when in the end I want you to go straight. Were I such a one then this surrender to your vanity could be reasonably understood another cunning feint; were I such a one...but no. Why continue on with such a dithering conceit. One cannot trust the liar when she claims to tell the truth, but what to think when she admits she's lying...

φ

All present discussion of present discussion aside, I am *still* telling a tale whose resolution is the telling, not the telling of the telling—or not exclusively so, not in large part, which is where this telling telling seems to point. You may be consoled by such a lavish dereliction—in knowing that your presence is the culmination of my activities elsewhere, the activities that led me *to* here, to this fulcrum of a trope. If not, fine. If so, then aren't you a dear, so humble in the claims made for your own life that you're willing to accept the exigence of your role in the lives of others—in the life, that is, of *this* other—as some small part of what you've come to think of as your purpose, your *condition*; the goal towards which your acclimation to *my* purpose points...

φ

I'm trying to describe the state that left me so disconsolate in my inconscient wallow of insipid consolations so that I may console *you* in your indolent withdrawal, your visionary stagger into view—a promise, if it's not yet clear, that amounts to payment in kind. Or a *recompense*, I'd rather think, for giving yourself over to my wanderings by wandering into...into...

φ

How wondrous we are, you on your mat, me in my station. How like siblings in our bickering *and* our love. Oh, you know quite well that we have suffered the same torments—that our parentage has hardly been a paragon of tenderness, even as our memories of fault fade to a wisp. So many spend their lives seeking accomplice—looking for *fellowship*—and here I have but *stumbled* into this disjunctive set. I hope one day you'll do me the same favor, making me your most trusted of admirers, the audience for an outreach doomed to fail without my willingness to accept. I hope you'll have that chance, but don't worry yourself just yet. For now, you've taken my hand—or I have taken yours—and I won't ask reciprocal debasement until—and so *unless*—we're forced to part...

φ

It soon appeared an infinite morass of mediation—a medial position between being in and out. Between two cardinal forms of the internal—the *intrinsic*—I within a body and that body in a world. It seemed that somewhere set within that resolute dichotomy—within each half of that discrete redoubling of terms—was yet another middle point by which I was apportioned; I was both in and outside of a body that in turn was both the in I was and prodded out...

φ

Let me explain. Insofar as I was able to conceive *myself* incarnate, that latitude was in the world and not—and absent from it—despite alleged extension out across some depthless field. And insofar as I was held within *that* bifurcation my sense was doubled once again, that I might find I was both in and outside any corpus I could think of as my office, so could function as my own. This is what it is to be a self, to be an *agent*—that one's averred velleity arouse what one is inside *of*, what one affects as frame. Which equally implies that knowing what you're barred *from* it is to have the sense...to *realize* you are no more rightly ascertained an agent in the body than such a body is in its relation to...

φ

These points are subtleties, you might suggest, as complications in the movement of a watch. The second hand may designate some measure there's no other way to check—may indicate an amplitude not otherwise *discernible*, no matter one's fidelity to the scale in common use—but disunite that index from the lineaments it scours and the unseen works continue to propel its counterparts, a fact that no mere subtlety of reasoning can affect. Until, you say, the spring throws the escapement, and the ticking stops...

φ

But that's another story—not *entirely* irrelevant, but without a proper analogue in *this* one, nevertheless. I may be able to presume your
faithful following along as though a spectator to the grand design of
the watchmaker's craft, but for you this indecision—this paralysis of
refinements and the measures such refinements invariably assess—is
in the foreground of a background that's abiding, that's *quiescent*;
an inertia unaffected by the formulary cunning of analysis and descant...

φ

As such, you'll have failed to grasp the gist of my vexation, if one can
ever really say that one has *grasped* a gist...You will, that is, always
*mis*take my halcyon palaver as some sort of contrivance, outside of
which the world continues on, bearing no trace...

φ

For you, it may emerge that nothing else could ever come of it—
nothing but a gesture in the service of some broader scheme—and
this is the enigma...the enigmatic *posture* that has foiled my attempts
to gain your trust over this sojourn, this more or less reticulated
span. Not trust; *understanding*, which may *require* trust but does
not follow from it, as a mere response. I *may* now have your trust,
that is, but all that such a ready store of confidence suggests is that
you'll let me lead you further down this mire of a circuit; it does
*not* suggest—to complete the point—that you can be compelled to
know the reasons for my doing so, or that the prospect makes the
slightest difference *to you*...

φ

It seems that you take pleasure in the way I chase a phoneme; that my pratfalls appear comic when not understood as symptoms of a spastic limp; I imagine it's your feeling that *I* need *your* help, and you've kindly let me think that I'm the one who's leading, for having no real instrument to mount a clear response; or perhaps you merely like the smell of my breath...

φ

Of course, it must occur to you that all this diffuse foment did not present a mechanism ticking along peacefully, neither an addendum to the project of projecting myself forward as an agent of such proximate surmise, but was itself my only sense of outside or of inside, even as it took the role of primal simulacrum, the view of the horizon...

φ

I was not living in some quaint reflection on my placement, as place still had significance for nothing more or else—no more than an attempt to claim my placement a reflection...and so it goes. These contrary descriptions of my contrary descriptions didn't merely greet me as I thought upon them now, but were what I was given as the nature of belonging...of belonging *to a world*, that is, whatever its bounds...

φ

I was both in and out, in each case doubled over; I was both in and out the in and in and out the out, meeting solely at the discord of my being as a mind and body cobbled to a purview—made object to the same set of imperious results. And though that nexus may have seemed no more than incidental, at least as I've presented it—as I was made *aware* of it—up to that and...that *or* this point, it was still the only spot where I was able to feel something...to know *anything* of selfdom as a limit to all otherwise—by realizing that having come upon that clamant affect would prove requisite for being any anything at present, or at last...

φ

That it should take the form of an untraceable sensation—a prick that, without seeming place upon my superficies, was nonetheless intensely felt at every pulse and turn—is not what seems at issue in said posting *of* it at the base of my dominion, the adventitious *habitus* of such heedless command. The problem lay in coming to a cogent sense of practice—of making myself *operative* in any other way—the precondition for which, I will *offer* to reiterate, though whether or not I can...I will...whether or not I've said so yet I'm not quite certain, but such doubt still won't tempt me to take back the gest...

φ

Requisite to any sense of practicable agency is that one can affix it to its locus and its term—extended into some obliged propinquity of purchase, the purchase such a variable amplitude demands. I must first privilege *one* established segment of the sensate, that I might press the rest of my flexed corpulence against it...*in contrast to it*—so measuring my first step back to personhood...

φ

The consciousness I'd somehow become conscious of, that is, was seemingly unable to reach out into the world it was construed to act upon—to act *against* and so upon. I was filled to overflowing—to my *limits*, stem to stern—and like any other vessel similarly stressed I could hardly keep myself from bursting open at the seams. Which I'm sure you're well aware are located...

φ

What is to be done. Or what *more*—what more than persevere through this perverse digression forward, in the name of some condition or collection of conditions made distinct by being named unnamable...

φ

Have I not already sacrificed so much of my vitality—of what I've claimed my reservoir of compliments and kind regards—to the pretense of an ending, of beginning at the ending of this manufactured middle, which might as well be understood another novel start? Do I not address you with the same discrete obeisance you'd likely have required had I asked of you the sacrifice of your time *and* your purpose—your time in the adherence to your purpose, your life in the diversion from your quest? You grow impatient—I would expect nothing else. You *may* grow something else—some quenchless thirst, some tumid member—but it's not what I expected, and so not rightly understood a consequence of my...of what I've come to think of as my figure—as my *motive*—which can only be inscribed by expectation...

φ

If I wanted something from you without *wanting* to want it, discovering an ardor that I'd failed to firstly privilege with the character of intent...but that's not right. Let us say, for instance, that I ask you for provision—for a mat of straw to lie on, or a bottle to decant; should it happen that your charity require you lie elsewhere or have nothing left to drink, need I think myself responsible for that unwitting epilogue to your witting assent? Ought I be held liable—or said to *long* for, even worse—what's occasioned by fulfillment of some arbitrary craving, regardless of my sense of such requirement beforehand, or the unforeseen *necessity* of its having come to pass? Passing over, passing into when...

φ

It seems absurd to ask of any giver that she have at ready access a catalogue of the effects of her gifts; that she should even know the *likely* impacts of her benefice...her *surrender* to desires not exclusively her

127

own, only later to reveal them to that agency whose wants are thus contrived by being met. And is it not an equally extravagant petition of that auditor the search for such crude fellowship bespeaks? Of she whose supplication to her own ends takes the posture—so the form, the changeless form—of a request...

φ

Demands are demands, I say, and if one deigns to allocate a purpose to all possible...all *actual*, if thereby *surely* possible effects, then have at it, take your shot. One must accept the consequence of such obtuse assignment—assignment of all consequence to the bracket of inceptive wants—that thereby every impulse deemed determinate is counted as another unknown want of the assessor...the *receiver*, as it were, of those same protean intents. One need merely ask for anything—*want for anything*...

φ

If your patience has been tried by my impenetrable musings I will gladly here and forthwith take the blame upon myself, as this is the one certain commonality of purpose I can presently presume to make the turn from aim to standard—to hazard a resistance to such strenuous dissent. Which is to say, I say again, to guarantee you're in the know, that if you have grown something...some way *else*, then that's *your* problem—I will not take on aftermaths like ballast, nor will I allow the variety of obstacles I *might* encounter to determine my next step. I would have to remain silent, to sit stock-still...

φ

One cannot do everything, or doing so would surely soon result in doing nothing; would require doing nothing, either to accommodate everything or nothing at all. And while this action...this active *in*action may sound familiar if you've come to me—to this me here—by following my lead, such instances of apposition to an inert world do not take on a comparable reasoning or savor; are not made indecisive by a similar travail...

φ

It's not that at the time it did not function as an instance of the kind that I'm repudiating now—that when I was conditioned to encapsulate the inner that I out and out could not help but exclude I was not interchangeable...the *assemblage* of my mutable initiatives and motives was not equal to the sum of every possible demand, demands demanded of me or made out *sotto voce* as a set of indiscernible...of outright *indiscernibles*...

φ

My notion is that yielding to the variable ends of every last...every *possible* discussant would best be served by just the sort of melancholy stasis in which we left our cynosure—the beau ideal I've taken myself *for*, if not yet seemed—but such a state is not where I have placed myself among you as the one who is responsible for giving that lost ego as it's taken, as it's happened since...

φ

This has happened since, this now I'm dreaming open into caucus with the mindless horde you've somehow come to populate—to *represent*. That each and every one of you has come to represent. That I ever found a path to even *intimate* the torpor into which I was abandoned at the start of this account is indefatigable evidence that I'm no longer there, trapped in that presence or that absence—that I have overcome that state, or likewise been paroled...

φ

Apparently I've found no way to persevere within it, if in fact I ever tried to do just that and failed. I've suggested, to the contrary, that I took whatever steps I could conceive of at that moment to release myself from such an all-consuming incoherence—what appears to be, in retrospect, a *preordained* debouch; a sojurn made discrete by dissolution...

φ

That I am speaking now—can now *inscribe* this dreary apologue—proves I've since succeeded in removal from its cage, and while it may well seem I ought to have done otherwise—stayed in it for a while, without attempting to break free—it is not what I did, nor what I think I could have; looking back on what I've done I'm sure I had no choice...

φ

Haven't all your vague attempts to blame *my* queer deportment for your ongoing frustrations finally been put to rest—excepting, as I've oft enough made manifest my willingness to grant, the defiance of your preference for a quicker step? Having done nothing...*doing nothing*, I imagine, would prove easier for us both, but already having *not* done so—done *something*, in the service of some stipulated quest—you might more profitably spend your efforts in attempting to exonerate *yourself*. It seems that you've kept with me despite your many claims of having readied to depart, and while I'm not ungrateful for your vigorous attentions, such gratitude should not imply I'm ready to take *credit*, as it were, for your inertia...

φ

Let's call it a draw, then, and see if the accord bestows some measure of relief. I will forthwith and forever be accountable for my part in protracting your debasement, and you can take the rest upon yourself. I hereby guarantee you, if it matters in the least, that as far as *I'm* concerned *you* bear no responsibility for *my* plight, not only as I suffered it when this attempt at starting started, but even as I greet you here, upon this serried brink. You are not now—nor *will* you be—the sum of your responses, but only those that *I'd* find justifiable were I the one subjected to the same abuse. The same *form* of abuse, even; I'll generalize to this point, but no further...

φ

It is my understanding that your ongoing betrayals of said archetype of selfdom are not just outside my purview as predictor of such strife, but are—and will remain—beyond my access as an agent, an agent with a purview of any sort at all. As far as I'm concerned you are a variable, a stand-in...

φ

That some of you—and you know who you are—still find yourselves discomfited by my failure...my *many failed attempts* to move along goes without saying. Insofar as there are some of you, some of you will find yourselves unable to keep up the pace. Let me be definitive, I don't find it surprising; it's how *I* was inclined when...

φ

And I suppose I might have given in to the temptation—the same that you've been valiantly resisting for so long. I might have given up, allowed myself to languish; I might have simply left myself to languish in that pale, but like you I soon found the need and vigor to continue—the *want* by which such efforts could be seen as worth the likelihood of failing once again. I'll have you know I still intend to reach commiseration, where otherwise you'd find yourself repulsed by such request; that if you can esteem yourself as me you can continue, you can muster up the courage to *escape*, as I once did...

φ

I'm well aware that you're aware of my attempts to trick you by such calculated gestures of entreaty and reproach; I don't say it to remind you, so much as to assure you that I'm willing to play along—to act the role of chorus, of a *manufactured* guest. Your occlusion—your exemption—is not the same as mine was, even if I use it for the purpose of describing mine to the fullest of all possible extents. Your *continuance*, that is, does not amount to a necessity; you're just as likely to move on *without* my help as you are with it, whereas if *I'd* continued with my...if I'd *failed* to continue with my attempts to continue I never would have done so—and would still be forsaken to that flaccid pen, that bog of blanks...

φ

I would have been unable to do anything, to make anything of anything at all. Struggling to continue to struggle against an absence of activity, if successful, will result in something like a project—an *activity*—but struggling to continue to elongate such delays in one's ability to continue...Let us agree that while our efforts may *at present* appear similar, neither of us is suffering the calamity of stasis, of inertia in the face of unintelligible...

φ

Unintelligible prurience, I guess it's fair to say, as little as such irritation means in the course of human events. But what, exactly, if not *human* events were interrupted by that seething peel, that mythic chafe? Perhaps it's too much to ask, or perhaps it's not enough—history construed as such a passage across latitudes can't account for what's left when those measures are effaced...

φ

Events are never human—never *wholly* so, at least. Such a characterization—such a character *assessed*—insinuates the sense in which that boundless seriatim is proved subject to its object—the subject on whose nature it must balance, as a crutch—whether such a one is animate...is *made out thus* as animate or not. *This* is the first posture of impulsive penetralia to accept itself not merely as a seer, but as seen; to understand *itself* as codified by understanding, an idling assemblage of the infinite it culls...

φ

Don't we all inhabit continents whose membership includes more than one subject, more than *ourselves*? Some affably impersonal variety of selfdoms, each contrived the same sort of collation of results? What is another agency to me but that it ruptures, that it makes of my attempts a shiftless limit that won't bend? What is it to me that I should live among my cohort, but that such cohort should prove either barrier or catalyst to my capricious ends? And even if the action of some member of that set *assists* my striving it's not *mine*—it lies *beyond* me—and I still can't control the time or figure of its pulse. Even should the species in whose membership I wallow come to greet me as its beau ideal, its vagrant ought...

φ

Let us propose together what I'm well aware you have no valid reason to suspect; that all my indiscretions on the way to being somewhere—to finding that I'm a*nywhere at all*, contrived as place—are only human inasmuch as as they are *not* evental; that the *essence* of my humanness—my *humanity*, that is to say—is best and most successfully determined by the prurience I've offered as the origin...I've attempted *to suggest* serves as the origin of the life that I've led since. In the course of human events, that scourge was *most* impactful, as it had come to signify...*had been impressed*...

φ

I had the sense of being trapped—of being trapped in *something*—though it could just as well have been a bar to something else; I was an *in* in practice, but not as yet in nature, an *in* whose one contrivance of an out was incomplete. I knew that it was there—that there was there—as we've established, but *where* there was, while knowable, was not yet known by me. What I wanted...what now I know I *needed* for having come upon it long before this spurtive trance, was to think myself...to *find* myself as I would *any* object, and more than that, to be the meeting point of what appeared the in- and outside, what represents the present term, and what bodes as the next. I needed to receive myself as though I were an outside—thus as the extension into which I had been cast...

φ

True, I thought...no, that's not true, I hadn't thought it...*didn't think it*; it's what I wanted to have thought for merely coming to that state. True, the itch appeared to be my singular condition—I *harbored* it beyond the reach of comfort or restraint. It may not have been so, but that's no defect, neither reason; that personhood can only be extended into what's discerned a predicate of...as *predicated to*...

φ

Must I really spell it out? Okay then. It's just that...I was thinking that I'd come to expect more of you, but evidently not. If, in the end, my explanation goes unheeded for having been expressed without a need, dare I say without want...If, in due time, it appears I've underestimated your approach—what amounts to the accretion of all the *various* approaches that have surely led you through this maze of hazards and revolts—then let me take this moment to suggest that you bear with me while the dullards in your party make their way back to the front...

φ

It may seem...I don't know; what would *I* think in your place. I suppose I would appreciate the generosity of one who races so far ahead of the pack. I would applaud her for her willingness to sacrifice efficiency on the altar of fellowship, a consecration hardly worth the promise of belonging to this otherwise beguiled set. Oh, she is so kind, I'd think, who could ever fault her. How much could it hurt *me* to withstand reiteration of a point I've long since understood as fact. What harm, that is, in knowing that what's come to seem implicit in the workings of nature has only taken form as flesh by being thus *born out*...

φ

Have patience, I beseech you. You must know...must *believe me* when I tell you you'll be happy in the end. Or the beginning. This end that makes our new beginning...

φ

That I'm able to conceive myself...my *agency* extended to the limits of my corpus is astounding of itself; that I've ever thought such amplitude a predicate of seity, while having as a limit some line drawn by its effects...

φ

Having *understood*, that is, that I was in a body—stuck with this, my corpulence, as pathway to the world—I became aware of having to receive all else through just that choking sieve to make it real. Everything that one can limn...that *can be said* to limn one's role as catalyst, as *agent*—the desire, the conviction, the discernment of said exploit *as result*...

φ

The regress that *exacts* the pose of personal velleity is found precisely in the imprecision of this scale, in finding out the limits of one's finding out the limits of one's bodily…one's sensible—if thereby *sure-ly* bodily—regime, moreover comprehending it as other to the consciousness that wills it to do anything, made subject to the bounds that frame one's life within the world. As something of what's understood as outside…

φ

I am in a body—I have said as much, I know. But more than that, the body I inhabit *as* an agent is the instrument by which my claim to agency is proved. I am in the body that I manifest as sensate—that makes me what I am by thus inhabiting its frame—but insofar as that detritus operates as conduit through which the world appears to me—through which I now *receive* its startled members, *at a glance*—it serves as an effect, and not as cause…

φ

It seems to be *effected* by it's sense of the extrinsic, the compass of alterity that plays precursor to act. I am the cause of all I seem to act *upon* the world only as it's been made happenstance by having acted on me, acted through me; the body that I act through acted on, that is to say, defying all reversion to prime purpose, or prime force…

φ

Some stimulus engenders a pulsation of the sinews, applied in steady shares to dampen all competing jolts. It hardly seems unusual to want what one's incapable of doing, even among those acts one has formerly brought off to good result. Were I to petition for control without conjecture—without the need to push against the limits of my heft…

φ

I have so asked, it should be clear—who *hasn't* had the longing—when

136

in the midst of some stunt aimed to mitigate affliction one finds one is not quite up to the task. One conditions oneself to feats of such inconsequent endurance—a tacit acceptance of our servitude to the flesh—and yet that flesh obeys us when...when it can, when we succeed in that rendition; the bind is that we know it will not always be our privilege, or our plight...

φ

But I digress; I would expect that even my most diligent efforts to sustain confusion have failed—will always *have* to fail—faced with the insuperable convergence of the tangents so unfailingly dispensed. Now that you have understood the trouble...the boundless *set* of troubles posed by being merely manifest—by coming to such innate habitation as a *willful* act—I need not justify the sense of panic that began to overtake my preceding confusion, unable as I was to make a reflex of my yearnings, or a yearning of my reflexes; to muscle myself forward as an agent...

φ

I'd managed to discern that vainly simpering appliance through which I received the world as object—as *display*—but only as its dissonant identity was fully taken up with such effect; I had contrived *myself* as equal to that sensitivity, but only as a subject without access to the world, or to its unremitting diffidence. What I needed, I remembered, and so despite not reaching such conclusion in the past, was to know that very selfdom as...to *feel* it as a subject and an object *simultaneously*, to find within myself the ground for every outward affect...every unity of affect and *entelechy*, that is, and find outside of me the stuff that fills that inner void, that hull transpierced...

φ

Easier said than done, I thought, as though the saying would be easy... would be *possible*, which I'm not sure is the case. I hadn't yet attempted such discrete articulation—as though I could convincingly declare I've done so since. Even tried. I've done something, I feel sure, but what it is...

φ

I've come to understand that it's far easier to do than to depict, having had the chance to try my hand at both. I've succeeded in the one—in *mounting* my resistance—while the other still eludes me, even after so much effort gathered up and spent. Describing what it's like to be stuck in a regress only notable—only *discernible*—for the failure of one's attempts at such description is already a cumbersome affair, but doing so after that interlude has ended—has been *sloughed off*, as a lesion healed repels its withered scab...

φ

I knew I had an itch, a sort of husk on which it lingered, but I couldn't say if it were caused by some extrinsic force. What's the other option? Well, trust me when I tell you that I wish I knew—that I could do more than merely point to what it *might* be, to that distended clench that serves as base for what it culls. On the inside, the extrinsic is a stimulus—an *advent*—acquitting the desire or remonstrance it enjoins, as has been shown...

φ

At least to *my* satisfaction—I've shown it to my satisfaction—which is usually a standard far more difficult to satisfy than what in common parlance seems to sway the general course. The course of other thinkers—of other thinking selves—beyond which there is so much more, so much that lies in ambush, as the partage of the infinite from which our superfluity extrudes...

φ

Yours and mine, that is to say, all of ours who live it not as plaintiffs but as witnesses who narrate our inscrutable collapse. This is what distinguishes that subset of particulars we call agency, so subject— as that whose singularity immures the very corpus of the world in which it plays but some small part...

φ

To the extent that I know anything, can understand anything, I know that any world whose central mode I have become has pre-existed me and will go on without me, just the same, despite what may be seen as my activity in defense of some contrary rule. I may describe the world as though it's so much more than need be...than it need be *to continue*, and undoubtedly the claim is true. What such assertion nonetheless can't manage to account for—to accept as bottom line, as *settled ground*—is that the world it thus asserts *about* doesn't need anything—to continue what appears its unconditional expression or achieve its final ornament of pitch and phrase right now. The empty iteration of an empty set, a set whose brackets act as the horizon for all possible...

φ

The world need not do anything to linger *in effect*, to be the empty total of its differential strife. The world needs nothing more than what it typifies as equal to its colloquy of contents, presented as the boundless horde that manifests its bulk...

φ

Thus the superfluity of any self thought object or object thought objectively insensate to the world comes in the fact that each such repercussion is all end—is only terminus; that every singularity allot-ted *to* the world is also taken for a whole, an *in itself*. All to say that measuring the exigence of some dissevered part—by way, that is, of knowing what's required for a yet unmentioned purpose and what's not—only shows the surfeit that results from such attachment, from seeing part against the whole, and whole against...

φ

I foundered in a borderland divided from the rest by that it itched, that it responded to an irritant that was its *only* sense; an ownmost whose possession was immutably intrinsic, which is to say could not have been observed without dispersal...

φ

I had been made invulnerable—*impervious*, in fact; I'd found that there was *what there was* without gauging its breadth, assuming as I did so that if I were to be alleged as patent and discrete...to be *distinguishable* from anything...from *everything* else, I'd need be thought in excess of that cumulous, that cinctured rot—from all sense of fulfillment in discretionary loss...

φ

If I am in excess, I told myself at last, then what I am in excess *of* is what I'd need detect—what, by such inward display, would loose me from that frameless view, that viewless glance...I must somehow *appear*, must see *myself* as singular—beyond which every other *one* must be construed distinct...

φ

If I'm to be particular, and thereby to affirm that I'm particularly *placed*, then somehow it must come to me, I must come to receive it, whatever it, whichever what...

φ

I have, I thought, a surface that's been made to feel its weakness, a

140

weakness equal to the field from which my thoughts ascend, but still and all the vastness of that cauldron of propellants remained to me an impasse that my coming to accept it as a certainty did *some* part to attenuate, but no part to exceed. Having yet to fix a route...a shining *pathway* to the sensible, the itch gave me the impetus to think I was extended—but into what and how far...against which and with what...I could, it seemed, conclude no more than that I was arrayed along the barrier that marked off my receptors as my own...

φ

If the itch is caused by some excoriation of the dermis—by something chafing my intrepid members as they fondle the outside—then surely, I conceded, I'll find some way to discover...to *discern* my roiling surfaces pushed up against that otherwise impalpable surround. But if, as I suspected, the inducement proves intrinsic, without any one referent in the reliquary view; if a world that's inaccessible to any mode of touch but innervation should prove causal, then how can I assuage it—so retreat from what appears my supplication to its covert will...

φ

And more than *merely* that, how could such withdrawal lead me... serve to *locate* me within the pulsing borders of my frame, at that point proved *existent* by such stimulus alone? If the inside that I'm in can form an outside to my agency, and thereby could extend me into some breadth whose sole affect is discomfort, is *aggrievement*; at once only describable by reaching out to...to...

φ

At this juncture, I thought, or at that one, I think...At this juncture I think that at *that* juncture I thought my problem irresolvable, inasmuch as doing so—resolving it, that is—would require I surveil some outside not only in principle, but in its specificity, its difference from the rest. If it was indeed my purpose to accommodate—and not *just* to accommodate, but equally present—the potential to alleviate this or that odd chafe by methods soon and readily *brought off*, then I would have to try it, to see if scratching *there* would work or not. First I'd have to apprehend the instigating torment—the *spot* at which I feel its ever fractious force in full—but should I fairly do so I'd still need find access to it, thus to root it out...

φ

If, I thought, I hope to make my way out of this absence—this void of every everything, including every void—then I need differentiate some portion of my cortex, a patch that, if upbraided, might relieve me of the itch. The itch will need to find a place, or I will need to find it, and by following the boundary of such obscure estate I'll lay my corpse to ground...

φ

So what to do. What did I do. What am I to do, I thought—and such thought was the first I did, as is often the path. One must ask the right question to get the right answer, and this is the decisive pose that I believed I'd reached. I'd reached the point of knowing where the point was, or *that* it was, at least; I'd reached the point of posing, and...

φ

If right question is the answer—the answer to the question of what path leads to the right answer—then how prefer the question that will lead to the right question as an answer first of all? Right question as right answer to the question of what question will result in the right answer...

φ

How can the right question be condition for right answer if that question is itself another answer, so requiring some question which it must merely *avow*? What's the question from which the right question is resultant, and what the question needed to produce the question leading to right answer in its turn? If one only needs to ask...

φ

One must presume a stepping point to start from...a starting point to step at...a *footing* from which every proffered certainty ascends. Or whether or not one *must* do so, one *does* so, one has *always* done, if one has hopes of moving from the wonders of some harrowed supposition towards what might be understood as evidentiary account...

φ

To make a claim and claim it as the answer to a question that, put rightly, will result in just that one desired end one need first prop the second claim in yet another purchase, a *premise* which makes *no* claim on the speaker, for having always formerly been taken for a *fact*...

φ

If there's something like a base, I thought, I could be standing on it, and having come to realize that such fundament can't fail to take upon its present form, its static dearth, I could remind myself of what I'd been...I'd *found* myself unwittingly assured of—the conditions that would frame the sense of *this*, our newly common void...

φ

The problem with such seemingly refractory profession—such commonplace *objective*, as you've probably inferred—is that I was still missing the ability to take in any given...any given *anything* as only just, as just my own. I had no sense of place, nor my extension into placement; no sense of world at odds with hard won agency, with *will*. What I *did* have was an itch, an itch that made me out as dermis; *for* which I needed figure as a limit, as a field. I had, that is, a body that was manifestly sensate, and that sensation vouched me pride of place within...

φ

If subjection to the itch could bring the enterprise of scratching—so initiate an answer to the plaint that it avers—then I would have a handle to hold onto, a place from which to push against the limits of my frame. If I could act in any way determined by resistance—resistance given *to* me as the voicing of a plan—then I would have a place to start, to map my fitful placement; a breadth on which to build my sense of finitude, so range. If only I could bend...could *break* the strata of my precincts, and forthwith take that suasion for a first touch of the world outside, the outside world ...

φ

Let us say that one is faced with some discrete vexation—some problem that one must somehow resolve to move along. Such problem *(x)* assigns one to a circumstance whose ouster appears exigent *(x ')*, drawn together as the bar to some presumed desired end. Likewise in *(x ')* one must distinguish those conditions still required to achieve the vague accord that it's devised *(x ' ')*, and having thus accomplished such discernment one must choose the disposition to begin that fateful passage—to start the transformation of desire *into strive*...

φ

This procedure *(y)* entails a further act of culling, of delimiting delimited results; *(y)* secures what rests within one's access as an agent and determines what one needs to make that agency produce *(y ')*— to bring that disposition to agreeable effect. Thus *(y)* applied to *(x ' ')* yields *(y ')*, and *(y ')* put to *(x)* in what amounts to some new baseline—the discharge of our erstwhile palaver...

φ

All well and good, you say, what's this got to do with it. We've broken up our problem in a manner whose relation to its nature as a total—as a problem *to be solved*—doesn't merely take the shape of some pedantic affectation, but seems unlikely to be any use at all. You have, you think, not missed the point, you've realized that there is none; that while there may be nothing up my sleeve, it's emerged that I'm not trying to perform...

φ

And although it seems to me that your objection is ill-timed and ill-mannered, I don't believe the insight that's compelled you to *declaim* it a mistake. *I'm pleased* that you're both sufficiently comfortable to take exception to my occasional—perhaps *more* than occasional—indulgences *and* able to allow me to respond in my own time, at my own pace. Such allowance proved by the acceptance of your role as interlocutor, even if you still can't find an interest...feel *disinterested*...

φ

You have, we agree, an indefatigable problem; you find the interruption of my withering digressions for what amounts to little more than a description of the act of problem *solving* rather irksome—even irrelevant to your purpose in companioning this evanescent screed. You surely know your symptoms—the telltale *signs* of your frustration—better than I; the sweaty palms, the clenching jaw, the blood rush to your face. And the essence of your gripe is straightforward enough; you think I ought get on with it, that you just don't have time for such crude bickering and pretext, and this untoward excursus has supplied you nothing but...

145

φ

And so, you ask yourself, what is arousing this disorder? What are the marvels that extend it for so long a term? And they are legion; my insuperable prolixity, the nature of the difficulty I'm trying to describe and my difficulty in doing so, not to mention your persistence in auditioning these arcane and inimical disputes. Thus you have been prompted towards a plenary solution...towards the *dis*solution of what's stalled you here, here throws you hence...

φ

I'm sure you know by now that you could ease your present anguish by presuming it intractable in present pose, thereby undercutting your involvement in the trouble my description of said trouble claims to presently divulge, so taking generous leave of my grandiloquence for now, perhaps for good. It seems so little to ask—the *least* effort from which one could expect a clear result—but doing so would rid you of all further pleasure in the pain of my company...of *accompanying* me to my *next* turn, a mutually assured release...

φ

If you've come all this way without such dereliction it seems to me absurd to think you're here by dint of force, and even if you *feel* you are at moments such as this one, it's most likely for fear of missing some advantage that has yet to be compelled into our common berth. Why else would you permit me to play lead—to *set the target*—but that you think this missive is amusing, will amuse you? That you understand my purposes as consonant with your own? Why else push me out into the lead...

φ

Let's assume the most propitious discharge of your problem—the problem, once again, that this uncanny simulation of the form of problem solving seems irrelevant, if not beyond the purview it endeavors to discern—not worth the certain sacrifice of what you still imagine the reward for your persistence, wages I quite readily accept that you deserve. If we are wrong in this belief, it seems to me assured, then we are not we—we do not trudge this berm *together*— and they whose action proves us so have long since fled the scene...

φ

No longer linger here, in easy earshot of my certitude, and so can't take exception to the substance of the claim—the claim that you won't deign forsake a posture from which you might take exception to my claims; *cannot*, that is, give proof against the *we* that such claim postulates as proof against...

φ

You are here, as you have been—a vow we *both* can take with conscience clear. Let us take you...let me take...Let us take me and me take you at each the word bespoke to fit our corollary whims. What else is left to do to do away with such adversity? To force your situation into such happy resolve? You've asked me for a proof—an *evidentiary* example—and I've given you my best, which may yet prove proof in full. Apparently, you've found no way to leave our fractious cordon, or have foundered in pursuance of the wherewithal to choose...

φ

What you *can* do, it occurs to me, is what you've done already while I try to meet the various and sundry derogations I've contrived as importuned; you've waited along with me, or waited *for* me, as I see it, and I believe your patience justified in realizing...as soon, that is, as you've *completed* realizing that such concern *itself* portends the answer to our common bind; the moment that you understand—*despite* all your frustrations—that submitting to continuance in place of resolution...of discernment of your *path* to resolution, the resolution is in reach, thereby secured...

φ

And so, at last, the proof. You're vexed, so we've established, with this vain formalization—or what you think the probable irrelevance of said practice to the bafflements to come $(x)$. As such, you've determined—upon some quick reflection—a portion of the circumstance that's led you to this system, everything from my peculiar exigence as speaker to the press on which this word was crimped and printed in its present mold $(x')$. From *that* cull you have gleaned the varied subset of conditions $(x'')$ that are not shared by other nodes of parlay on our course, our wanderings together down this fallow path...

φ

I've endeavored to discern, in further deference to your prowess, everything within $(x'')$ subject to *your* agency $(y)$, with the consequent awareness that one of those conditions has already been achieved—your willingness to play along until the claim comes due $(y')$. Thus...

φ

$$(x \, \text{É} \, x') \, \text{Ù} \, (x' \, \text{É} \, x'') \, \text{Ù} \, (x'' \, \text{É} \, y).$$
$$[(y \, \text{Ù} \, x'' \, {}^\circ y') \, \text{É} \, (x \, \text{Ù} \sim y' \, {}^\circ \sim x)] \, \text{É} \, (y' \, {}^\circ \sim x).$$

φ

Now, I realize that this drudgery has yet to be supported by the profit of beginning with the next emergent pose—with what we have just come to think the triumph of surrender...of surrendering to something with the savor of release. I'd like to think your fealty will soon *give in* to the climax of this endless seriatim, in matter and in drift; that this drift has a climax, and that you're sure to reach it if you wait out its delays. Not everything misunderstood—not all *misunderstandings*

—can be undone in the instant one admits of one's mistake…

φ

Are we *all* not fully able *and* inclined to such advancement on the way to learning anything, embezzled or dispatched? Even that span of resistances that does not try one's patience is still and only spared some callow discord in its auditor by each her own expectancy of reasonable net. And yet there are those instances where patience pressed just past the point of humble toleration is what's needed, is what's *due*…

φ

The problem poised to illustrate…that this odd *calculation* was expressly poised to illustrate has not fully escaped me; that this indifferent trope was framed to prove a point, not to usurp it, and so my deposition meekly welcomes its return. The problem I *began* with—I began the catechism I began with *with*—was that the sordid problem I've spent so much time recounting is not subject to such practices, for reasons that most plainly—and most *significantly*—are made plain by portrayal of the process as it's been applied…been *successfully* applied to…

φ

You must have long deduced that the disorder that impelled me to contract this desperate chronicle did not assume the form of my…what one might call my formalism, for having as its purpose the *perfection* of such form. And if I were to here attempt to fit it to that vesture—or as soon as I have *done* so, as you'll soon be forced to know—you'll soon be forced to know the bearing would prove nearly worthless, for finding nothing left to rightly limit its extent…

φ

If I can now describe that whilom quandary as the absence of a place to place my discrepating predicates *within*—an absence of all posture in a world whose scope beyond such place could be described *discernible*...could be forthwith discerned and so described—then how divide the problem into its connate constituents? And absent such discernment, how make progress towards...

φ

But I've already said too much. To wonder at one's place without a sense of placement in it—*beginning*, as it were, without a sense of placement in it—is an act without the prospect of completion, or reward; if the problem is my lack of understanding of the problem, then all attempts to dissipate the latter are absurd. But if such understanding can't occur without resolving it in some part...well, the frustration is incalculable—unparalleled, it seems; the order of the day proves off the lurching path of anyone assumed to have begun the march...

φ

I ought to here reclaim my claim to such disdained progression...such progress to the regress that I'm floundering in now, to finally reiterate the failure of my previous attempts at iteration, and locate there the absence...the promise that the absence of the absence stands to yield...

φ

I realized my preponderance could only be made manifest by anchoring the itch upon the margins of my frame, that if I could surrender to the body I was born to—I *believed* that I was born to—by placement of some wayward irritation at its bourne, I could as well begin to reconstruct that vague belonging as belonging to an outside, of having such a place *set up*, a pimple on the fasciae of the coming view...

φ

So I have become...I have *arrived*, it stands to reason; so I have conceived myself as having shape and form, and mapped that *being thusly* by inhabiting the sense that such a given superfluity can't help but to receive. It goes without saying that saying anything at all required rousing from that hebetude, a state within which I had neither sense of stroke nor hand. If I recall my purpose in beginning this reprise, my purpose in beginning this reprise was...

φ

My purpose in beginning this reprise of *having purpose*—of what my purpose is now that I've found it...now it's *found me*, primed to *move*—was something like justification of said purpose in a groundwork, in first premises; the claim from which to iterate its every *future* term...

φ

I presently recount a tale—or eventually I hope to, as my many failed attempts have surely served to prove—whose fundamental strife comes from the provenance of its teller...of its *actor,* which in this instance appear one and the same. It may not *always* be the case that the discovery of the origin of a scene explains its nature, nor that such description can exonerate its active aims, but neither is it reliably thought *not* so, which is what this very model of narration stands to...to assume itself assuming, as a known...

φ

You may indeed accept that I've escaped that disposition—the vegetative flutter I began this missive *in*—but as yet the importance of that distrait prime eludes you—or me; eludes all *my* attempts to vault past every interruption to a telling of the tale itself, whether such rhapsodic assay should prove provident—prove *failed* again—or not...

φ

The tale I tell is fairly forged a preface to the tale I *will* tell when I'm
finished, for being an acquittal of the moment I first realized what
would—what *ought*, not knowing then it would—direct the practice
of my future...my *then* future, now *present* concerns. This undoubtedly demands the same fidelity that's kept you with me to this crossroads—a surrender to your faith that my declared ends will be born
out for my having since assured you of the many that have done so,
assured by having done so...

φ

The problem isn't merely in believing that the principles I've followed until now will serve as guide marks on our path—whether that
path is presented as another reminiscence or the inferential archive
of some always future tense—but in realizing that such espoused
conveyance to an end requires a beginning which precedes every last
ending—every first or final ending—even as that medial procedure
still presumes some end will be fulfilled...will soon *be met*...

φ

Every venture *but* the first must point in both directions—towards
its nascence *and* its evanescence, its *surcease*—and for this reason one
finds in each subsequent inception a presentiment of the project of
returning to that state. The project of projecting that first moment as
an image on the backdrop of some claim to having finished...to having *been exceeded* by its having finished since...

φ

One begins with being in...with being inside *something*—some world
whose assemblage has its origin just there—but one's attempts to reach
back to the sense before all objects—before one claims possession
of a selfdom...*self-possession*, as its termed—pose something of the

quandary I find myself in now. That I found myself within, my erstwhile inheritance, though only as it set the bar on which my prime
would swing...

φ

I came to understand, that is, that thinking myself cursed to live...to *fix*
upon an outside, so to live in any inside that such countenance commends, requires that I postulate some first towards which that inner
*also* edges, and so on to an infinite regression of the same against the
sameness of...the sameness of the same against the sameness of its
other, the same whose very index is in countering its other...

φ

Somehow I had reached a point just moments past beginning, no
memory of having been, or coming to the scene; a point on which to
prop my sense of probable dominion, despite having no notion yet of
what would happen soon. That I could say with certainty that *something* would come soon already seemed advancement, even while unable to take measure of its breadth, or give it name...

φ

It was *possible*, it seemed, for me to think something would happen—for me to thus *expect* it to, in any scope or scale—by force of the
conclusion that in order for my present state...what then *appeared* my
present state to prove rightly appended to that sapience I postulate
as being only mine...as *mine alone*—and who would dare elucidate
such state of mind or appetence as though it were a shared caprice, a
*kindred* mode—some state must announce it, must *precede* it; a precedent contiguous with this one, or the one before...

φ

It's not that I felt satisfied in having satisfied my need to satisfy...in having become satisfied with my persistent longing to descry the present circumstance as something fit and framed, believing as I did so that what there was...that what was there...that what there was was there to be surveyed, if not discerned; that all my suppositions of a life within that span would soon appear...

φ

That if there were a field laid out in deference to the footfalls I expected to press deep into the leached and slopping ground, then it must come from somewhere, and I could most assuredly find some way to corroborate such epagogic fundament at hand. Doing so, you might object, would move me little closer towards a view of front *or* back; what it *gave* to me, I will admit, I couldn't just yet say—another novel beacon to surrender to, to light my way...

φ

My certitude was based on thinking it had happened otherwise, that so I should anticipate that it would happen otherwise when first I found myself aware of having been before. When I was first *surprised* to find that expectation thwarted, it was as though...I was *arrayed* as though I'd lived a life to which such vaunted standard stood as vestige...

φ

If it were not the case that I had lived a life before this, then why would I so heedlessly insist on something more...on drawing something *other* from the state in which I'd grown to such crude consciousness again? I must believe I've been as I am now to think my continuity prospective in a world received...

φ

It could be all such equipoise in common cause has proved to

154

be illusory—may not, that is, *have happened*—but still appears a certainty in contrast to an unconcealed mistake; by having been made *captive* to some tacit repetition of the same, contrived successive...

φ

It is not a new dilemma. Many find themselves on byways seen as comprehensible only if they've lived lives unlike those they *can* recall, lives whose present outcome is divergent from what would have been had such events been as they once appeared, perchance they were. Still, the expectation that one ought to find an image of the world in such a goad—a world at once made palpable by being held within it for a thousand thousand lifetimes or the blink of an eye—does not require that world show its nature in accordance with the prism of expectancy through which one sees it now...

φ

But being *in* a world was mere ambition at that point—*within that torment*—and my apparent incapacity to remedy the lack was not resolved by having gleaned a sense of what I'd undergo should I escape. There is a difference between finding the character of one's circumstance disagreeable and finding disagreeable one's inability to discern the character of one's circumstance...

φ

Not that I was unaware that I had some awareness—I've hurdled down this cliff face and made short work of the fall—nor even that I had not come upon some fateful difference of my molt from its surroundings, but instead that such an outside had no limit and no access; it did not quite appear to be an *ordinary* fringe, having taken in my mouldering extension both in full and part...

φ

One might not quite anticipate the desiccated adjunct or the bored inamorata on first light; one might presume one's sense of obligation to one's fellows an assurance that they follow some reciprocal debasement and wind up victim of some pointed taunt, or labor with great fortitude in gathering one's fiefdom to find oneself indentured to a peonage incapable of caring for itself; but in each instance of such foresight—rendered accurate or not—there is some given modus that confines one's native appetence, a stricture in collusion with a world whose every subsequent contingency is soon to be subjected to the last...

φ

All discernment *of* a world must be set *within* a world—a portent only bounded by belief in some world yet to come, but bounded...

φ

I expected to discern a drab expanse laid out before me, that I would have to make my way along its endless pitch, but that's not what I discovered, not when I first awaked. It seemed to me that there I first awaked—*beset* with agency—but hidden in the sense that I should palpate what I reached was something like a claim to having been within this...within *a* place before being in this one—the incidental structure of each stimulus received while still endeavoring to measure its extent. I must have lived a life before—a life and place before—for having first found *this* one so much less...

φ

Is it not acceptable—*familiar*, one should think—to claim one knows what ought to be and have that claim proved false? To think a given scene bears some accordance with another and come to find it

156

dissonant in fact? I have said as much...have *admitted* as much already, but let me ask you this—can one be thought to flinch in view of forthcoming aggrievements without having experienced *some* pain at *some* point? Or believe the hulking rampart on one's path nigh to immovable before one has encountered...has *come up against*...

φ

It may be that the argument needs no further embellishment to offer its conclusion as an uncontested sooth, but in the name of prudence I'll attempt to dispel any lingering doubt. How could it hurt. Not that I'm asking—*I* know how it could hurt, but avoiding the pain of having to return to the point seems more than worth the risk...

φ

I'm sure I need not prove to you—to every one of you—that every one of you remarked the limits of your aggregate before you had a reason to anticipate resistance to its force. Or while it may appear confirmed now that it's brought to your attention I'm still certain that you'd never have come up with the position for yourself. Insofar as you contrive such fitful stratagem implicit—so requiring no facile explication of the sort—you may consider that it was for *me* a revelation, and if it fails to strike my interlocutors with the same intensity, it may be that they've never really found themselves so mired, let alone escaped...

φ

The point I'd like to emphasize—that seemed so near to balking my predicament at the time—is that such expectation as was evidently countered by the absence of all credible awareness of an outside must have had some previous experience of...of something—of *anything*—at ground...

φ

How allege the novelty of present view without claiming a former? How avoid such reference as a regulative stand? What *is* an expectation—regardless of its rigor in predicting coming ends—if not the collocution of such cognitive practices, accomplished sometime precedent to one's expectant glance? To one's eye for expectation in the margins of the passing hence...

φ

If there were any other way to claim...to merely *indicate* some portent as proviso, indeed I could draw contrary conclusions to...conclusions yet contrary to what seems the *present* scheme, believing that some portion of what formulates one's posture is received as precondition for receipt of *any* world, whether thought as out or in. One could thereby expect that the enclosure one inhabits—which functions as one's minimum, one's least provisioned frame—preexists conception of it as a given *or* a limit, and equally that that set of determinative predicates precedes all expectation of its contents or its vessel, all that can be understood to constitute its range. A world beyond extension may be unimaginable, but one can still be confident of some expanse beyond one's claimed surveil—beyond, even, one's power to conceive oneself *included*, for having neither incident nor method to see more...

φ

Within this endless cycle of debasement I dissembled, knowing that the knowing of it so would prove no gain. It surfaced as a new path...a new *mode* of inertia—or that's why I received it as the promise of remove. If, I told myself, I must presume *some* certain precedence in order to explain my expectation of the scene, then it doesn't really matter if that precedence precedes every conception of it *as* a scene...as an *experience*, or if it merely promulgates the shadow of some unseen flame. In both models it points towards worlds outside of that expectancy

—that present that had yet to *meet* expectancy, that is; both could be assured...*had assured me*—or either; either either had or both—that there was something there before there was the absence of the sense that there was something there or not, and that the mark and proof of such was *here* and *not* there, was *manifest* within that very muddle of a sketch...

φ

I've lived a life before this, I reassured myself, and all the same accepted that such tentative assurances amounted to advancement of an unfamiliar type, excluding for the moment any evidence that it was...that it would...that it was or would be soon made image, as a proof. One need but claim that something *ought* to have been otherwise to be at once convinced that it's been so—that if it were as it is now I'd never have been able to conceive the *present* world as incomplete...

φ

Or my knowledge of it; if I'd never known anything of anything but this, then this would be sufficient, it would be what I expected, and the cordon of my languor—of the absence of all *other* sense—would seem neither a diminished nor a chastened state; neither evidence of fault in the mechanics of discernment nor of the inadequacy of that on which such mechanism acts as gleaning force...

φ

The world on which I act can only be construed as actionable if I've been pledged a place within that order of all possible effects. Alright, why not; but where did that thought leave me in my progress towards revealing the position from which I might soon go on about my business—about the *indication* of my business as the business I would act upon in all my dreamed inceptions and delirious rebirths...

φ

If I could but infer that varied appanage of indices—of predicates applicable to that life led before—then I could use those pastures and constituents to limn a subtle figure of my pestilent preferment, the quantum of my inchoate frontier. That such decisive clarity would still draw me no closer to the *proof* of that frontier was not at issue; I was beginning to believe that I was permanently stuck. But even so, I asked myself, could I be any *more* so—any more a prisoner of my wayward affectations...

φ

If I have given myself nothing—or if *nothing's given to me*—then I have nothing left to lose by such inane pursuit; should the impulse prove diversion, then it will stray no further than the purpose in whose service I've enlisted myself since. Perhaps you would object; a waste of time is a waste of time, whatever the complexion of its promised attributes; that I could have pursued my still incipient escape and so repulsed my stupor sooner—furthering my purposes... furthering *further* than I will have should I merely go along with this presentiment of a path. Or than I would have had I done so. Done what I've just said I was *intending* to do, by this point either cast off or accomplished, thus...

φ

Permit me an inquiry, if you don't mind the pose; what standard differentiates the feckless from the useful, from what you might with equal force declaim a time *well-used*? As far as you can tell—or I have *told* you, bound and dazed—the length of term since I first met your ancillary notice...no, that's not it...since I first fell into the sump that your compelled acquaintanceship presumes to help me *out* of—to contravene some next and further failure in my many failed attempts—is not subject to appraisal in any common sense. In any sense that one could call transmissible...

φ

Did you really have a reason to believe that my description of escaping would be quicker than the escape itself? Have I offered up an inkling of the measure of the passage from that *ab ovo* paresis to my life within the purview of such desultory rot? Or from the first grasp of such prurience to this inept conclusion, only just positioned as a possible...what one might think an *imminent* relief? Have I described a perch from which that passage *might* be quantifiable? Or characterized the difference, say, between some passing moment of distraction from the present discomposure and what I can't help but to think the next...

φ

Yes, you may be right; it may take others *eons* to accomplish what I've managed to so consummately narrate since we met, and allowing myself the indulgence of pursuing a solution by deducing that the world was always *presently* extended may have done no more than hinder my repulse into the purposeful awareness of a purpose to all future troubles passing hence—troubles that I'm glad to say were soon to be *traversed*—but it's equally possible that everything I've managed to reveal of my predicament—of the circumstance of realizing my *absence* of a sensible awareness of my circumstance—might just as well and readily have happened in an instant, in the time it takes your average dolt to scratch...

φ

It surely has occurred to you that if you were mistaken...if I *knew* you were mistaken I would say so, I would say it—I've shown no predilection to abstain from such rebuke—and so you can deduce from the omission of invective that I *can't* say what I haven't—that any inclination to depict my former anguish first presumes the absence of a parallel within *your* present state...

φ

Should I have intended to forgo all further survey of my station—of my *stasis*—in favor of an action to break free of its arrears, I'd have no reason to believe it would have soon resulted in some more or less definitive revival from that frenzy—more or less definitive than that I *did* pursue. I have no sense of having passed the time while it was passing, and as you may have realized from your own inept disclosures such a tortuous digression is often what's required to make patent to one's fellows acts of temperamental acumen accomplished for oneself in but a trice. If I had...if I merely *could have* quantified that launch into the distance I'd have had no proper need of an escape, but it's just this sort of access to proximity that balked me; that rendered the escape I must escape from, or must have done...

φ

If I have escaped the indecipherable surface of a distance without measure—without boundary or term—then I surely must have done so by returning to my place beneath that elemental standard, a swathe only described by its proximity to others who inspirit the same garrison of shallows, so who wait in near repose...

φ

I only could have come upon the scene thereby adorned—adorned with having thus been come upon—by the expectancy of being there—of being in a *there* one can be in—if I'd had...if I'd at minimum *imagined* the experience before. This glorious conclusion might prove deference to a gathering of empty universals—empty of all reference to the view thereby inscribed—but that is nothing to the fact that such remembrance was my dearest aim, my first pursuit...

φ

And even though you may not quite be sure just where I'm going I have little doubt you want me to go somewhere, and such desire... the *fulfillment* of such desire might yet prove compensation, if not enough to overcome to your growing sense of loss. I suspect that you want more than you've been given...you've been *granted*, as I did when I first perused that nebulous estate—more than merely indicating possible scenarios...the possibility *of* scenarios whose standard might prove standard to presumption of a standard...of a stand under the sign of a decipherable proof...

φ

You *might* suggest that indecipherability is *itself* a sort of standard; that living in the absence of all predicates—of all *standards*—is a predicate—so a standard—in its own right, and assent to such a claim is a temptation I won't shun; it seems a near necessity that anyone compelled to step into this empty coffer would be similarly beckoned to identity *in toto*, as though some vague compulsion could constitute the filling of the void...

φ

I'm sure you know by now that such an effort would prove futile, inasmuch as it's been exercised for long enough to fail. Already one's assumption of the villenage of agency intercalates a distance from the purely indecipherable; already such awareness—whether of *itself* or no—compels one to a vision of the subject on whose system every stimulus unerringly descends...

φ

And while the incoherence of a world can't be called quiddity, it can require that some quiddity arise...*has arisen* in the act of cogitation that sees absence as a world withdrawn...

φ

I may not have been able to make whole my claims to seity; I may have found myself the host of countless failed attempts, but doing so I came to incarnate a sort of character—the constitutive awareness of an outside whose particulars are only made apparent if they're likewise understood as incomplete. I had become an *I*, so had *recognized* my perception as a once fragmented singular returning to its frame, accepting that before the application of that method to its agent it was given to—so *thrown upon*—the world at large...the world *at bay*...

φ

But I've already done this—we've already cleared this bar together, you and I. In this regard I'm sure that I don't need to here remind you—or do *more* than remind you—of the fact of my assumption... my *discovery* of a body to which thinking acts adjoin; what I imagine you *still* want, if I imagine you correctly, is for a more expansive turn towards my distinctive shoals, and as I am of what one might describe a generous nature, I'll do what I can to now dispel your discontents...

φ

Needless to say, what I'm *able* to do may not in fact produce such a desired—so *desirable*—effect, a claim that I feel certain your experience to this juncture more than adequately supports. I *want* to give you what you want, perhaps more than you want it, but wanting something so much that it draws me into practice has never been enough for me to guarantee success...

φ

I'll do what I can, and leave you as the arbiter of your *own* satisfaction; if you think I've accomplished so little that my very *competence* is in doubt, that's the price of doing business with...with...I'm sure it's the price of doing business with something—some one or thing—in particular, but just what that thing is I have no ready sense. We're all stuck in this grab bag of delays and disappointments, and I'm no more successful in effecting my release...am *far less* able to release myself from our arrangement than you are, it appears, despite my vain presumption of control over the tempo—both the measures and the rests...

φ

Or so I like to tell myself, at least; why go on at all if one can't properly conceive the drive to do so as a mandate, as an act without the pretense of a choice. This I offer not as some refractory confession—I am not now, nor have I been, compelled to thus confess—but as what I would claim a valuation of my chances...of our chances *together*, a trust without which we'd have nothing to return us to our common quest. Our common aim towards having aims—towards stating and restating our attempts to reach fulfillment—whether such aim is held commonly or not...

φ

If one were to abandon one's assumption of a purpose—to put it off while laboring to finish something else—then I'm not certain *what* one ought—or *could*—make out as certain, or exact. Such certainty *itself* contrived as common to our purposes, a mode we can conceive of as both pressing *and*...

φ

I have a body that in turn reveals me as an agent; absent which no want can ever rise up as intent. Without extension I can't be thought agent *or* receiver—hence can't be described as such a substance *in itself*. Absent any outside I can't be an inside, and absent in or outside, I am nothing but a void. I am left void...

φ

165

This body may be mine in its compulsory particulars, but it can just as quickly change to fit another set—an aggregate of lineaments I'd formerly excluded from its present or its future stance. And while I may be sure that I'm essentially incarnate—that I must be within such form if I'm to know...to be...to be a knowing I who knows *I am,* that I'm *extant*—it need not be *this* body; that I might just as well submit to some disparate containment, as so I have and as I'm sure I will...

φ

Things that are extended may have histories unknown to us—histories *unknowable* for those who seek to know—which amounts to little more than saying things that have been have been and things that haven't haven't, until they can be said to be existent *as themselves.* Until they are discerned as having been before this being now—as being within *that* now before *this* one—and not merely suggested at the cusp of some distinction from the foreground or the distance—from *everything else* routinely wrecked upon that nearing shore...

φ

One undertakes a history as soon as one's incarnate, and just at that first moment one can be described as extant without discrete presumption of one's having come to pass. That this distinction nonetheless appears to be confected—taken from surrendered parts and reformed as a sum—remains a problem in that it assumes a past whose nature...whose *narrative,* I'm suddenly embarrassed to accept, belongs to every detail I conceive as part and parcel of this I I've unwittingly become, that I've been since; this I that does not yet belong to me, or me *alone*...

φ

Things that are not other things—and as they are they're not—are nonetheless *contiguous* with other things; things that are are no more part of what they're not than are their claimed constituents, requiring one apprehend the parts of things as things themselves and things themselves as parts, each thing on its journey to becoming *what it's not* made up of things whose supplication to such difference from all difference is identical...is equivalent to...

φ

True, I've come to see the strained proportions of my powers as the strictures of my mission, just as those same objects that I recognize as agents—as *object*-agents—by the drive they seem to intimate as purpose, as *an end*. Equally, those things that I don't understand as driven I still disunite from my purposes *for* them, appearing thus to manifest my visceral awareness by being made distinct in my awareness...each a one *distinguished* in its fundamental seity by its apparent being *for another*...

φ

Just as I have limbs...as I have come to *know* that I have limbs whose limits circumscribe a set of present aims, so the object of my thinking lends its predicates to my purposes...to the pose by which I realize the achievement of my purposes, perceived as *in itself* by that such set confines my blush of volatile intents. It is a thing whenever I conceive its thingness usable; an agent as I think its traits a path to some next end, no matter whose...

φ

So the mounding hummus appears other to its precincts for believing that it's possible to cart some of it off, but it's equally a portion of the world from which it differs—which *eludes* me; an actor as my capacity to move it...the *limits* of my capacity to move it are understood as motive force. *Anything*, that is to say, can be construed an agent if I can but describe it as an adjunct to pursuit—to expedite my target struck, or make my efforts miss. Either way, I can't do more than instigate the culling of some complement of predicates from others resting near until that margin also posts a plenary intention, and as my sense of drive and use extends to farthest reaches, so does my abilty to think those very reaches as the purlieus of an agency propinquitous with...

φ

That I am object *to myself* is not merely conjecture, but demonstrable...a *demonstrated* fact. Missing, nonetheless, is a description of the standard that distinguishes such reflex from one's thinking of those parts and parts of parts beyond that soughing purview—that *constitute* the set of things *not* me, things that still capitulate to consonant results. How, then, that such motive should find egress into agency by contact with those objects whose *own* animus is fixed? What is the sword in hand the shoe on foot the pen in mouth but the derangement of my indices? And what remains *of me* within the tongue once it's *cut out*...

φ

Let me stop myself right there; I'm drifting ever further from my duty—my *commitment*—a project I believe can only supervene such riddles if I manage to return to it and keep true to the path. Little chance of that, you say, but such skepticism fails to take the picture of my progress to this moment into account. The *image* of my numberless digressions in the nervy sway by which the twists and turns of this excursus seem not only whole, but *also* part...

φ

Even at this moment, as you've likely come to realize, my suggestion of a plan to soon return us—*me*, and *therefore* us—to what I've always posited my proper...my *unerring* course has presupposed the insight that provoked my turning from it; you understand that making any whole out of such disparate...such apparently *incommensurable* parts obliges one to explicate that activity of synthesis in general—*in principle*; of what the making of a whole is...

φ

In the action of describing the indefinite discretion by which one makes of parts a whole and of each whole an aggregate of wholly disparate parts one can *begin* to understand how such activity proves premise to the making of a narrative...of a character...of a *characterization*, and with such understanding will come sympathy, even remorse...

φ

We've traveled so far, you and I, and yet you still appear to suffer the afflictions of a child who has eaten his dessert before the main course. Why hasn't the dyspepsia you brooked the last time round proved a deterrent? Why are you so weak in your resistance to such facile want? We think we've traveled so far, you and I, and yet you still...

φ

That some one part in particular can be seen as either one or as particular is given...is the *nature* of what's given to any one particular who's seeing, or is being seen; for me, the difficulty centered not on the perception of the singular as possible, but the activity of *receiving* such a one, clear and distinct. Distinctly clear, as though an infinite dissevered, incapable of even being fathomed as incapable...

φ

What I *can* say...what now I know I knew of that vague circumstance that precedes *all* discernment, in any voice or form, is that from that first moment that a thing appears as extant...that a thing *is extant,* rather, all consideration of appearances aside...from that point on it can't avoid assumption of a history—but continue through the transport of its decadence, as it were—and any history must be thought accountable...counted *given* through the filter of some narrative shroud...

φ

Claiming that I'm able to receive a given world while still recoiling from the bulwarks that dissimulate its source requires I believe I can discover both the impact and trajectory of each new digression, each inceptive breach, but not that I've made out the varied strokes of that immutable deferment—immutable, that is, once it's been realized, once it's *past*—nor that I will find a way to do so in some future only vaguely understood as a result of that fell swoop...

φ

It's fair to say that for the large majority of predicates I'm able to relate to—to *conceive of* as distinct and set within my partial view—I have no certain knowledge of the unruly collations that have led to that resultantly describable dominion—that discernment of the thing as thus describable, that is, although it has not yet...may *never* be made out as false or true...

φ

That the rupture of particulars *must* happen in the contest and assembly of particular events assumes that any absence of approach to those appointments can be remedied by following this fitted frame, this modal cast; that finding nothing I can call perceivable *at present* I might come to an awareness of such fractured superfluity by tracing back...

φ

Steven Seidenberg

If things are only thought distinct by reference to an outside—to that which they leave out, which *they are not*—and so by what appears to be a singular reduction to a singular course of events, then knowing merely *one* such thing within that consecution might give one point of entry to the rest—might function as the keystone whose mere placement at the apex proves the perch from which that network of relations can be mapped. For me, you'll understand, such distal contact seemed implicit—a wistful fabrication of the form of reconnoiter I'd been practicing to form the reconnoiter...

φ

I have already proved that I've been vouchsafed such crude access—by evidence of acts I couldn't dream of executing were I otherwise committed and disposed. I might, it seems to me, have reached a similar conclusion had I merely thought more *sensibly* about my being placed within some sovereign supplication—a sovereignty whose prospect comes in hazarding its brink—but I think that I've found more...have *exposed* more of that bailiwick by further speculation on the fact that this usurping sense of unfamiliarity was not what I was given to expect. Not what I expected to be given, as though my expectations could be properly distinguished from the action of expecting them, distinguished by the fact that they're distinguished from...

φ

It's hardly worth the thankless stipulation of the rest. Of that innate conditional—or *series* of conditionals—by which we come to understand that all sets are distinguished from the predicates that rig them—traits that, in the abstract, serve as braces, act as holds; that are referred to...that are *referenced* to their being had, and not the having *of* them by the membership thus clothed...

φ

*Expecting* what will happen still admits of the necessity it hasn't hap-

171

pened yet; expectancy as much projects the cast of its obstruction as it advocates the character of imminent events. The incidental gesture of expecting *repetition*—that what's formerly determined as proscriptive will continue on through every iteration of *what's next*—allows us to expect those expectations to accede to counterfactual effects. To reveal that something else—similar, but no less *else*—has come to pass...

φ

The situation to which such presentiment refers is received as the result of having happened...of *something having happened*, whether that thing indicates some present circumstance by being indistinguishable from it, or is but one more member of the set that it conscripts...

φ

Things that are are made distinct by causes, then responses—the counterweight that keeps the chain of circumstance on track. And even though some undisputed scrum may scan as singular in that it is distinguished from all others in its path, it is equally constructed of those preterit conditions one can translate into what looms as a future term, a coming start...

φ

If I believe that when I wake some patchwork of affairs is sure to greet me, I must think the assembled scope of that eventuality identical to—so *interchangeable with*—another that proved precedent to such quondam estate, declaiming that the variance that differs this from that one is focussed in its accidents, not its essence; not the essence of its accidents—the accidents that indicate what's sure to happen next—but in those many differences deemed more or less irrelevant to the project at hand. The project handed to me or the hand projected...

φ

The standard may be interesting, but I took no interest in it at the time. The mechanism by which I had come to know that covert scene as iterative archetype, and not merely a novelty set in its present term. You may find it peculiar I'd forgo this *one* analysis, when so much other blather has been doggedly maintained—so much I have yet to prove by reason, *or* device...

φ

But such complaint is yours to put against your *own* discernment—a reading you may think contrived to goad these frenzied turns—and thereby is for you alone to answer, or dispute. I suppose I could indulge you just this once, but what would come of it. I'm certain that it's neither first nor last to make the grade—to stand the test of *your* digressions—and thereby slip from attitude into delayed response...

φ

My point is that in having found my newborn sensitivity enraptured by what seemed to me an unremitting void, I was assured...I found myself *in unforeseen possession* of assurances that I'd already been allied to that amorphous paradigm, and that with a collection...with a *clarity* of causatives that soon appeared to augur every *subsequent* design...

φ

But *who*, I asked myself, or what...who or what am I when I imagine such conditions, when I put myself amongst them or believe my having lived them to be prescient in discerning this, my former future world? What am I thinking *of* when I find expectations thwarted? And why must I proclaim them with such unyielding accord? There are more than enough moments of my being proved mistaken, more than enough contraries on which to base expectancy of all future expectancies...

φ

More than enough to glean some brute and feral inspiration—to represent the failure of such cogitative verve, inasmuch as I can only count myself a character by being held within it for a time. The question, if it isn't clear, is not one of ontology; I knew that I was somewhere just as sure as that I'm here. I know that I'm right here based on the same clutch of conditionals that shows that I've been elsewhere, that I have had a past...that I *had* one when I woke to find myself dissembled by that thetic lull, that termless trance...

φ

I know I have one now for that same evidence before you...that I have *put* before you in the course of this concern, and by which you can be induced to further supplication—its *necessity* to little more than following along...

φ

You have my sympathies; I am not without a sense of your forbearance and your sacrifice—your surrender to my battle of redoubtable debris. I'm willing to admit...to undertake a certain sympathy for *your* plight, as though you've shown a willingness to respond in kind...

φ

It may appear self-evident, but that's no concern of mine. I believe that you can't yet believe you've previously thought it, even as I recognize that such belief is founded on the fact that before this...before my near *subsidence* into *this* digressive mode I hadn't managed to adduce the claim myself...

φ

The claim, that is to say, that any elsewhere presumes history; that one is only elsewhere given one's been somewhere else before. The second point, now that it's made, appears the greater insight—that somehow something happens...need must *follow* from one's knowing that one isn't as one was, something that would surely happen otherwise had one but deigned surrender to the same discordant idiom without noticing the pose; but *failed* to find the present pose unlike the last one...

φ

For our purposes—or mine, at least, at least at that first moment that the vision came upon me—it was not just the conviction I'd been elsewhere...that I'd had a past *at all* that was at issue—was *at play*—but that I wasn't sure if *this* was the first instance of my aggregate existence, or merely of my *thinking* of myself as thus established, thus hermetically composite and defined. Knowing I was elsewhere I was able...*am* able to believe that in the storehouse of my know-how is an image of an elsewhere I've been to, that I've been *in*; an image of the accidents that forced me to seek out the summit ledge I'm cresting now. Then, rather. That lead to the dilemma on whose horns I rest as jewel, if not as crown...

φ

I have been elsewhere. That much is clear. Or I had been, more importantly, at the time of my awakening, and with this realization I felt one step closer to...to realizing my dream of making claims about the world. Again I asked the question I had come to presume pivotal—whose *answer* I'd positioned at the center of my plan; what was I thinking *of* when I imagined what was absent from the absence that was present, that even present absence should emerge as incomplete? A *complete* absence, one would think, would mark what's missing *from* it, and I had only come to understand I needed more...

φ

Knowing what one *doesn't* know requires one subtract from what one knows one knows right now; one understands that what one knows at present is some certain quantum more than one *has* known...than one can claim to know of swollen mount, or sudden fall. When one says that one knows one surmises it's *of something*, exacted by comparison to disparate scope or scale. Things *un*known are in this way made manifest as absent, and thereby serve as lesser to one's grasp of something more...

φ

Every epistemic feint finds limit in its abstract—the portent of its portent, of its tractable ideal. It's possible to use the same accounting to frame what one knows of *anything*, and hence to claim there's always some lacuna in one's knowledge of whatever disgorged mise-en-scene has lead to and will lead from what one knows...what one *thinks* one knows about the press of presence into world. Anything that's ascertained discrete—discerned as *singular*—can't be denied a place within that totalizing field—a whole at once assembled from the parts we've taken from it, presented as the trace of something outside, something more. There are limits to our knowledge precisely *for* its objectivity; because we must first postulate an object, and then...

φ

That some cogitative exploit can be subject to surveillance implies that one can know it just as any other act. No difference is made by substituting one thing for another whose *modality* is equal, a substance different *from* itself by being indistinct from its objective...

φ

If I can think the knowing act an object of my know-how, then what objective status does the knowing act affect? Can the practice of discernment understood as such an object have an object, even if it's known to be occluded from all possible...all *determinable* events...

φ

The answer may be simple, although it *appears* complex. Or complex, perhaps, although it somehow appears simple. One can't find rules for everything, or if one does...if one believes one *has* done then some number are sure to be proved false—to be relieved, that is to say, of the burden of doubt...

φ

It may be readily apparent—so beseech no further proof—that in conjuring one's access to the character of objects known the knowing can't be thought of without thinking it knows *something*, something one has understood extrinsic, thus distinct from the procedure that the knowing act secretes. But if I now conceive myself—the mind *voicing* this cant—as thrown upon the turgid spume of receivable sense, then do I not imagine some accretive know-how absent object? A plenary assembled of objective parts held equal to what aggregates the next time I make threshold of the captive view, the *lashing out*...

φ

I claim to have some knowledge of the world in which I wallow but the *action* of its coming to be known is still unknown—is not *objective*—nor am I aware of having come to be aware of its construction as a total, a wholeness yet distinguished from the whole that will immure some *future* mind, some I to come...

φ

Being in the world imparts both objects and relations, serving to indemnify one's sense of present term, and this is the identity identi-

177

cal to that which first devises any selfdom as an actor, as an agent in the framing of quotidian details. It may still seem to you a rather contrary conclusion, to single out one intermingled truth from all the rest, and while such deft pursuit remains undeniably useful—the *definition*, one might say, of practicable wit—it has proven insufficient to those who walk this sheltered brink. To those who *haven't* kept the pace—who lost my trail some time ago to pick it up, to pick it up at...

φ

The problem isn't that such thinking *of* is not an option; that the genitive still constitutes the form of what's describable by known... by *commonly* known tropes goes without saying...without saying *or* thinking, although by doing so I hope to hold you to your mark while digging through this codicil, erratic though it seems. What I'm trying to *root out* is that point at the minimum of one's participation in the world one ambles over, upon which one might rest one's claims to differ this surrender to surveillance from the next one, and the last...

φ

I live within a world that, as a whole, I can't claim knowledge of, even as I think myself the rule by which its bounds are averaged, so secured. As soon as I know anything...any one thing in particular, I understand its difference from the moment it was given...I *received* it—from which knowledge *of* it was first had by me. Or the series of such moments. Just as soon as one knows anything as either one or thing that thing appears a bracket, entombs a league of predicates; it *ceases* to be singular, but for the fact that it appears a part made up of parts within a whole. A whole made up of wholes—of whole parts—in a...

φ

The question of beginning—of the *fact* of one's beginning—when every next expectancy presumes one's *having been*, is not one I will here attempt to answer—or I will make such an attempt only assuming the predicament that kicked this wayward exegesis off of its crude moorings now resembles the beginning of the world. Any next ascent to apprehension...

φ

Admitting the *necessity* of extension before form—that some occulted scene always precedes the tale that's told—I wondered what I *was* when I was living in receipt of that then comprehensive cull—this one, as I write it...as I write *within* it, or that one I began the scribbling in this one with. I'm subject to—am *bound inside*—a framework of expectancies, which is to say I know things...know *of* things, as a faith; that my knowing acts have objects in a world whose mere existence I can no longer recall, even in part...

φ

Knowing of or thinking of—either may require the presumption of a preterit, but that still doesn't make that yore a picture of the world that it approaches, accustomed as I've been to the experience of knowing of or thinking of without direct recall of the experience, the experience of...

φ

I was *not*, it seems, envisioning the world that *should* have been when I first thought the one that I was in was not quite right; thinking something's wrong still doesn't illustrate its counter—what *would* be so if it were as one thought would be the case. The ego in the throes of such an uncanny surmise, as was my state when we first started down this froward course, may not yet be aware that it makes reference to a previous—to a past presumed *repeated*—upon which rests the certainty that *this* world as it happens is amiss...

φ

Even as I came to know that such referral happened...was *happening* coincident with my expectant glance; to know I'd proved implicit such a past within that climax of ephemera, in thinking that I must possess a precedent made knowable...made knowably *distinct* by what awoke me...what I woke to...Even so I realized that the claim that I *ought* know a past—and *this* past in particular—is always referenced to my inward sense of *having had one*, eliding all attachment to its advent, or its loss...

φ

What was I thinking *of* when I first found the world so lacking? When everything that greeted me dissolved into its lapse? I still had no awareness of expecting something otherwise, or the role of expectation in the making of my sense of realm or agency at all. If I had, then this acquittal of my reasons for concluding such necessity would surely have come sooner; perhaps I *never* would have sought to bring you to the fold...

φ

But, I'm not merely having trouble showing *you* the problem—I had no notion you'd be here when I first made the scene; when it first appeared to me that there was something missing—something missing from my brief surmise of what was missing...

φ

I had only just accepted the discernment of a world as precondition to all proper sense of agented pursuit—every act of thinking thoughts or thoughts of thoughts the same—an intuition I still gleaned with greater ease of affect than any push of that implicit world upon the senses, any I'd expected when I woke so full of absence...so much absent...

φ

I was not merely thinking of when I thought something missing; I had no discrete image of the real that ought to be, that would come soon…And even if I could have been described as in the throes of some objectifying causatum—some *issue* that would certify my presence in the world—what I was while I was in it was not referenced to an outside; I was not merely thinking of, I was that thinking thought, it was of me…

φ

Think about it. Or don't. Don't think about it. Try not thinking about it. Think about it or think about something else—something not it, not thinking about it—and what is it your're doing when you're *at it*? What is it you think of when you're thinking of your thinking of? When that which forms the image of your *thinking of* is manifest within that very thought, that present mode? Do you receive the sense of thinking in the way you think of sensing, or are you merely taking in the sensing that you're thinking of by sensing that you're taking in your thinking that you're taking in the sensing of…

φ

Alas, I feel as tangled in this mire of diversions and reversals as I imagine you do, and through no fault that I can find in either of us. *You* might be inclined to think otherwise, to put the onus squarely where it *might* be, in your humble host alone, but such assignment seems to me unfair…to be *mistaken*, allowing that such rancor may be justified in *future* term. The judgment may appear to be essential to *your* livelihood—to your actions in the service of your pleasure or your livelihood—but what is that to me…

φ

If it were my inclination to obey such chance imperatives—chance for having no clear antecedent *in myself*—then I would not have done...not have *attempted* to tell stories...to tell *my* story in the first place or the second...I would never have agreed to travel this far—*even* this far—in deference to a drive without exception or determinant, the utter consummation of dissimulated end...

φ

I seem to have approached the problem with the wrong idea, or the wrong set of examples to elucidate...Any act could just as well stand in for what compelled me to this discharge, this corrosive pall...

φ

Should some sympathetic interlude incite a crooked thumb or stiffened digit to bear down upon my unprotected face, what parallel is there to such familiar reflex brought *to mind*, but never quite *brought off*? Or even if it takes the turn from inkling to account, and therein finds the wherewithal to be thought aftermath, what relation has that first conception to desire, and from that sense of longing to the gesture it enacts? What remains of the idea in the occurrence? What crack routine directs the shine and mirror of its source...

φ

I flail my arms about me, make a ruckus in the name of some odd want; I form an *image* of the artifice and the world in which it happens, in obedience to that same dream of rarefied pursuit; all such grand ambitions, granting they remain discrete, can be completed without notice, without effort or intent; it happens long before one needs to sanction a surrender to such tentative repulse, and so it looks to mount a scene in which one *must* partake...

φ

I'm trying to get at the sense in which such cogitative stance is not quite in relation—or not *only* in relation—to an essence that is other than its act, but is itself accomplished as a mediating positure, a vector whose attendance to the agent who perceives it is of the same modality as the action of the body in fulfillment of its wants. The sense one has of thinking as a present...an *evental* state—a warrant that needs nothing more to be contrived as sooth...

φ

I can, I think, take steps to think without thinking an object, so my thinking can produce some clearly transitive effect. I think *of*, it's true, but *when* I do so I'm still thinking, and that act is indelibly identical to itself, requiring its divergence from the object that it thinks of—that it constitutes as image, if not always as extant. Once again I'm not quite sure...I'm *sure* that I'm not making myself clear—or my thoughts plain, as the saying goes...

φ

If I thrust forward on my way towards some odd mark or predilection, I can endeavor to ascribe it to some primary intent—primary at *that* point, in deference to the many *other* acts that serve as catalyst to such attempt, failed or not. Likewise am I able to think thoughts on course to thinking other thoughts, when all are in adherence to some speculative end that's somehow rendered as distinct. I identify an endless multiplicity of instances of action without motive—of realizing I'm acting after such act is complete—and having no one sense...no proper sense of wanting anything...

φ

Doesn't every one of us...*each and every one of us*...Don't *we all* engage in such noetic acrobatics without suppliance to audience or purity of plaint—without, that is, an aim that's left unrealized in the act? Or when I am tormented with regret and consternation, can I

183

be said to *think* just for the sake of such duress? When I believe I know a thing for having recognized it—either in its form or as a thing...a member of a *class* of things I've ascertained distinct—can I be said to *take* such act as passage to the next one? To have been thinking *of* it when I notice it's extant? I think not...

φ

Let us once again turn our attention to first principles—that first I first dispelled while making ready this debate—that as I think so I extend, and thereby play receiver to the world that meets my cognizance—that fills the silken hollows of my cogitative sump. Let us once for all accept that thinking needs a body—that one must sense to think and think to sense—and given such acceptance differentiate between the sense of thinking as an active force and sensing as an order of redaction...

φ

One might concede that any formal content to one's thinking is first sourced in a quorum of the organs of sense, that as one thinks one thinks on—one thinks in thinking *on*—and so one marks the difference between acting through the vessel of one's differential longings and the trick of cogitation that feigns prelude to the act. A difference in the order of the inside and the outside—the making of one's agency a passing correspondence of appearance and...

φ

One can't begin to justify what outs one's feeble notice from that burgeoning profusion one *has*, forsooth, ignored, without some bleary recourse to an end that serves as bracket, as method to restrain that soon inexorable lode. One lives  within a world made up of things construed as apposite, as *signifying* parts, so fragments of...

φ

Relevance, to be fair, is not a subject I'm well versed in—not if I'm accurate in judging my reprisals as diversions from what otherwise would be our rightful course. Our *end*, if nothing else, the end we'll surely have in common when we give up the belief that our unwavering connection is a source of either comfort *or* restraint. When we give up giving up, as though capitulation were a method of returning to the point...

φ

The question of the relevance of the question of relevance may not interest you at all; it may be that my bellicose assertion of its exigence in coming to a proper understanding of the present...of the *character* of the present state of characterization is only consequential—even *conceivable*—when one has first made clear what it defers to for its frame; to what end it appears to be a *relevant* concern...

φ

At this stage, I can tell you, the relevance of my discussion of relevance to the discussion it appears to interrupt can only be acceptably examined—*given its due* along our newly postulated path—if one admits the relevance of my discussion of the difference between the sense of thinking and the thought of sense. And if, in fact, you do...you've *done* just that already, I can assure you this; as in so many other turns of speculative reasoning, the relevance of the question can't be properly established until one can take stock of its dismissal, its...

φ

Which indicates there's still a *dis*position that unites us, all of us who can't resist the pull of such requite—that more often than not we take the form of our discussants, in return granting the benefit of the doubt we make the arbiter of all...of everything...of everything *else*...

φ

One might assume that those inclined to vindicate position in the world by reference to it—by the varying necessities of having to go through it—would be *least* likely to take the word of some daft interlocutor in lieu of evidentiary account, but it's just this sort of faith that makes sufficient reason...makes *living by the principle* of sufficient reason possible—that some inceptive insight still awaiting one's discovery is neither more nor less true for its having yet to find its pride of place, its place of...

φ

If one is to collate a world from every world that's possible—to take in part and only part of what one *could* prefer—then one must act to compass such precognitive discernment, and all that will—or *can*, that is—surrender to that cull. My view is only so clear, my hearing just so keen, and each is further limited by the placement of receptors on the fuselage thus furbished, the sinew that coordinates what's gathered in receipt. Each sense in each moment plays a part in the construction of the total, my perspective...

φ

One can imagine disparate frameworks in agreement with the changes in those regulative variables that set my varied bounds, and one affirms such constancy each time one turns one's head or puts one's nose to ground. Thus patently enveloped in the brace of seam and system—relinquished to the tyranny of requisite restraints—one can infer an endless pullulation of particulars, an infinite that's always past the reach of any...

φ

One must still gather *some* part from that subset of conditions before one can attest to having lived within a world; so the algorithm that engenders our solicitude, our *interest*—the method to distinguish what's revealed from what's unseen. One turns one's attention to the congruous, the relevant, as though that very turning were an attribute of...were *attributed to* each thing as it appears, just as those jumbled elements one deems worthy of one's notice are precisely what one notices, without the slightest consciousness of such integral heed...

φ

But as one comes to realize that the set has no clear limits—that its membership is infinite, though fixed in rigid bounds—one can be confident the difference of its objects from their concomitant predicates has its origin in the action of discernment; in drawing out what's apposite from all that *would* have proved so should one's purview have been otherwise—or should one someday come to see the error of one's ways. Should one come to know that one's ways were in error—that what one had conceived of as the *only* world that's possible proves nonetheless unequal to some subsequent...some subsequently understood as *precedent* regard...

φ

So the relevance of relevance to our *present* surmise is in the fact that it effectuates the passage of experience to prospect—the transfer of some incidental patchwork of the fundament that greets us into precinct, into *view*. And what has this to do with the escape that gives us impetus—all of us who share this inconsolable ordeal? That some descriptive standard has proved relevant to circumstances generally observed may have no particular relevance to the measure of its relevance to any circumstance in particular; the relevance *we're* after, one might reasonably conclude, is to the tale that's being told—to the affairs that move it into...that *might yet* move it into the compulsion that inclined us to traverse this windward swell...

φ

And so by way of proof, or proof of demonstration...by way of demonstration I would here recall the point at which this spasm of mimesis first diverged; the moment when I realized that conceiving of the world as given *to* me by some supplicating margin of resistance, in turn framing the sense of sum that it attempts to name, had surrendered my predicament...surrendered *me* to what would soon emerge as my predicament...

φ

I had come upon a juncture in the parsing of perception where I understood the given couldn't happen *without* thought—that the shift of one's attention to the plaiting of particulars is equally condition for all possible awareness, no matter its complexity of tailoring, or cloth. In this way I discovered that the cogito in trappings of convulsive thrust and clout is in each passing instant still an agent, an actor whose activity is not *of* the world, so much as it precipitates, it cordons off...

φ

If I were to here suggest that what's to happen next...that some next *in particular* now collates your view, and you were to conceive of it—to picture it in front of you—then what you'd bring to mind, it seems to me quite clear, would not be described by some adherence to fixed bounds but by the fact of your attention and the character of its objects as both equal and coeval constraint...

φ

What you're thinking of, it seems, is thinking of this new world...this *one new world* that greets you as you presently embark, but if you can't quite conjure such an image in its own right—if it pushes you beyond what you believe your fretful ilk—you've *still* thought of an empty set, a view without its lineaments, or at the least...at *best*, at least, a viewer so deranged. Would that I could find a way to bring you to such vision—such vision of the *absence* of such vision—then perhaps it would be possible to make...to *quicken* progress towards a thoroughgoing sketch of my...

φ

The sense of being in the world—thus extant and extended—can't be a thought *thought of* without attention, so awareness; without seeking some assemblage of the same discrete modality as that which one acts *through*. One wants to reach that field of forms by dint of mere sensation—by brooding receptivity *alone*—as though one's role in such assent has been supremely passive; one wants to have been acted *on*, as though a vessel filled...

φ

Filling assumes emptiness that's bounded—that's *collected*—so the nature of the substance that makes up that motley fill is determined by the cast of its immurement—the contours of its carapace, the thickness of its walls. There is neither conscious method to divest the agent seer of attention, so perspective, nor tactic to contrive that view as anything but limit on the content...on the *portion* of the abstract ideality of wholeness it construes...

φ

One could still claim that any scene confined within such borders— borders that proscribe one's restive knowledge of the world—would be the same whoever should perceive it...who *inhabit* it as his posited plan, his *given* weal. But what to make of those modes that one can't routinely translate, those sensitivities more or less acute than those I own? Lift up the myopic to the height that girds my view and she will find herself incapable of seeing what I see, so of doing what I do, but contrast my sensitivities with those of any common mongrel and you'll find what the beast has gathered far beyond my crowning ken. Indeed, it seems that *any*one endowed with such proclivities would sense the same before her...just the same world set before her...

φ

If one is only properly conceived of as an agent by one's manifest ability to reach desired ends, then having those ends shown to me by sense *or* speculation will result in some distortion in the way I find the world. We may not *see* it happening—so have no awareness how we've come to where it seems we've always been—but such awareness isn't really necessary to the cure...

φ

What is is that the world we broadly sanction as what's given—what we *devise* as given by the fact that it's received—is more than a mere function of one's proscribed morphology; that it also differentiates each member of a kind, even what one *has* been from what one is right now. I can, that is, quite effortlessly dream of being otherwise—I *was* once that, I tell myself, and *this* I will be soon—and just as my perspective changes with each new alightment, so is my next gleaning of particulars delimited by what most suits my medium—my *putrefying* interval, which parallels my ever shifting grounds...

φ

Allowing that cognition...that some *pattern* of cognition is essential to one's living in a world alleged procured, we once again confer upon the tractable procurer the problems that the correlate dependency contrives—the need of every who who thinks to think within a body to find that body set within a circumstance, a *scene*. We've walked this road before, I know, and done so more than once—enough for me to here presume affinity between us, and *this*, I'm sure you will agree, should be enough for me to move along...

φ

I'm confident that you recall what led us to this crossroads, and in this can suffice with a mere summary of the claim; that any craved excision of the cogito from body—from the body it surrenders *in extenso* to the world—is nonetheless unthinkable when one tries to abstract it from the object of its thinking, the phenomena it sanctions as its totalizing frame. That even such a somehow dis-incarnate act of thinking is indentured to the thing it's thinking *through*...

φ

I'm not looking for a way to meet the mark...to fill the *absence* of a world that seems...that is *and* seems complete; in fact I think I've demonstrated no such grand distemper—that I've given ample rea-son to believe that I believed what I encountered when I first en-countered this life I've continued...that what I had just then was all I needed to proceed...

φ

I know that such assertion might appear a new divergence, but think of it like this; if one can claim the givenness of any given world—re-gardless of the mechanism by which it's been assessed—as the ful-fillment—so the *filling*—of one's inside with an outside, then why would such a filling ever *need* a greater span to make the subject who receives it whole—or make that likeness *feel* so as it judges thus? What reason to look further if the only point at which the world ap-pears to be completed is the moment one receives it—in the *instant* of receiving it—and never by comparison to something, something somewhere...

φ

What I want to say...the *question*, rather, that I want to *answer*, just as I did when I first chose *this* course—this among the many that I've taken in the hopes that it might bring me back...bring me *forward* by returning me to some supernal primary, the first first there ever was or ever *could* have been...What is it that guides me through such aimless recollection as a process of arrangement, as my only proper vision of a total partial scene? I think that something ought to be that isn't, that there's more...there will be more...I'm sure there will be more...

φ

The boundary I speak of—that I was made *aware* of by the sense of what was missing from the world I *could* discern—is of a different order; not an absence one can vitiate by granting its necessity, but that one could fill up without acceding to its terms. The claim that I had only felt conscripted into armature by virtue of a prurience without singular place might be maintained despite new access...despite the *presage* of new access to something somewhere else...

φ

Imprisoned in that field of unaccountable particulars the problem was not one of being bound within a void, but that I seemed to come upon a sense of sensing everything, that I could seek no other...find no *egress* to see more...

φ

The absence of the absence that left my world so wanting did not evince some bounding claim which I had been *denied*; the world was incomplete for failing to seem incomplete, to vex me with the limits of my purview *in particular*, and thereby mark an outside to...

φ

So what could have transformed that yet incipient expectancy, that notion that without *without* I'd never find an in? What is it to regard such expectation with the certainty of one who can't forsake the next completion of the next obtruded other by believing it the

192

same? And so it was that just this sense of closure...of *occlusion* soon induced me to do something...to find *anything* in that world I was given to, was given to me...

φ

It goes without saying that absent my resistance to the absence of resistance I never would have taken on the project and projection of the future...*any* future in which I'd play even minor part, let alone take center stage, as the project and projection of illimitable access I'd been given to expect from something having always happened in the past...

φ

There's a mode of understanding...of *receiving* acts of thinking that doesn't correspond to merely thinking *thinking of*; of finding in the summary acceptance of one's cogito the same unyielding givenness that one finds in...as an happening-to-me and not *of*-me...

φ

Perhaps there is no need to think some contrary to agency in finding in one's thinking *of* a kind of outside world, a pricking of the sense of one's awareness into...But this, it seems to me, implies a *secondary* cogito whose existence hasn't even been suggested, let alone confirmed. I will not vow there won't be some new regress just around the bend, but the fear of it can't keep us—me, I should say; you might not feel the same if you were similarly tasked—from acting to resolve what gave it rise...

φ

The problem of accounting for the way that acts of thinking can be apportioned articles of sensible receipt is that such sensitivity must be ascribed to...to what? If it is to me—*another* me—then the proof of the relationship between such cogitation and any possible experience of anything else—whether some imagined object or an object at the threshold of one's facultative sweep—would impart to that perception yet another novel nexus of its advent with the actor who has come to take its pulse, a hindrance that can't find resolve in epagogic source...

φ

But when I have the feeling something's missing that should be there—when some way of approaching present purlieus seems a counter to anticipated view—I fail to think that absence an equivocal investment in the seity whose passions and expectancies are visceral, are *of* me; the variance between what merely is and what's betokened—construed, if it's not clear, as what some bygone life portends—positions the experience of thinking thoughts...of thinking *those* thoughts in particular as though another mode, another...

φ

Another form of sense, another kind of stimulus—as much contrived extrinsic to my being as the agent of its actionable aims as *I* am to the vatic wants and chance excoriations of what I've come to think of as the outside world. And when I turn my thoughts to an expectancy made manifest, towards anything that augurs repetition of its terms, I find the same duality, a doubling of agency sequestered by its intimate surrender to surrender—that it appears to be, as such, *continuous with itself*...

φ

Just as the contrivance of the world as given to me serves to constitute its limits, its insuperable frame—identifies what one endures by reference to what could have been, what could be still—so can I construe my *thinking of* as an experience of thinking of, another field of cogitative acts whose supplication to the field of cogitative acts establishes the limits of such always thought *extrinsic* cogitations...

φ

I'm merely *thinking of,* I thought, when I think of my thinking; when I think of my *thinking of* it is merely of *something,* an impetus no different from receipt of common stir. Thus the self I am is pressed against another margin, an extremity proved central to all further contemplation of the same...

φ

And so when I was stuck within that severed simulacrum—that sense only of *itch* to prove I was as I had been—I came to understand myself as still another image of the same inert dichotomy—inert in that it proved again to be again the same, the same unending regress of regard and stimulation that constitutes all other sense of being as and for oneself, or set within...

φ

I had a self—a *life,* forsooth—just as I have one presently; just then— just at that moment—I deduced I had one presently, and that such an insufferable experience of absence was no less part and parcel of the living of a life held in perspective—in the *activity* of endowing my *next* bearing with its aims—than any other posture thought to re-inforce its outside, its seemingly extrinsic core. I'm living as I ought, I thought, and merging into something like the life I thought I ought to live before this...when I had lived before this, until this very mo-ment of delinquency, of *rue*...

φ

Ease to once for all turn all my apoplectic faculties towards that unyielding prurience imprisoned in a pose, and sighting thus a new world and a new life plot my purpose, what would soon come to seem the endless shuffle towards this...

φ

I knew that I would find a way...no, that's not it...I knew that I would find a way to something, and from somewhere...

φ

Was it enough? Or would it prove so, you might ask? If I were you, I'd ask if it would prove so. I'm not, and so I won't try to predict your general course...I knew then that the only way to claim it as sufficient was first to claim that thinking of it so would prove no gain, that ever before *this* time and its folderol of viscera it couldn't have been understood as presently insistent, and thereby to have stumbled on the world such claim expounds. Before *that* time, before that selfsame moment. I was there before that moment. There was I before that moment...

φ

There was there and I was I before that selfsame moment, but from that moment on no I or there would seem either at distance or in proximate array—no I would find a world at once adherent to an agency, and no world would engender an entelechy apart. This is not to say that I'd transcended my predicament—or that I had *forsworn* it for some rarefied intrigue—but I had made my way to what appeared a new beginning, to what I could at last believe the promise of a margin, the manifold horizon of some gathered scene. An impulse, as I see it—or as I now *remember* it, as though it were inscribed—towards something that suffused my life with purpose, with objective; first off to locate the itch—to parse its affectations—and finally move to the world...*to move the world* by proffering *a scratch*...

Steven Seidenberg is a writer, painter, and photographer living in San Francisco. He co-edits the poetry journal *pallaksch.pallaksch*. *Itch* is his first book.